Sweet 'n' Easy

by Hajra Makda

Dedication

To family and friends.
Past, present and future.

Hajra Makda has asserted her rights to be identified as the author of this work.
A catalogue record of this book is available from the British Library.

ISBN 0 9535617 1 2
Text Copyright ©Hajra Makda 2001
Photographic Copyright ©Hajra Makda 2001
Web address: www.sweetnspicy.com

In this book quantities are given in Metric and Imperial measures.
Exact conversions from one measure to another, does not usually give convenient working quantities. So for this reason the metric measurements have been rounded of to the nearest units.

Recipes containing raw eggs should be avoided by babies,
nursing or expectant mothers and the elderly.

Published in the UK by Tropic Publications, PO Box 5786, Leicester, LE5 5WL, England, UK.

Acknowledgements

I consider myself extremely fortunate to have been blessed with an ever increasing circle of family, friends and readers at a local, national and International level.

It was their genuine enthusiasm and valid interest which inspired me to write this book almost immediately following the launch of Spice'n'Easy, when I was inundated with requests to write a book for those with a sweet tooth, and for those who enjoyed entertaining.

Again I extend my sincere appreciation to my husband Ismail, and sons Rizwaan and Junaid, for their moral support and confidence in my writing, as well as in the culinary creations that I offer them on a daily basis.

I'd also like to extend my gratitude to all those of you who offered their much valued support. It is practically impossible to name each individual, but it's your imput that has made Sweet'n'Easy a great pleasure to write.

Project Editor Hajra Makda
Book Design Garage Design
Photography Helen Mcann

Gratitude cannot be measured in ounces or grams but only in silent prayer. ©Hajra Makda

Introduction

I was extremely surprised to hear innocent comments from colleagues of their perception that Asian sweets and desserts were "sticky" and heavy halwas. In turn they were equally shocked to discover that we prided ourselves on our own recipes and ideas, for traditional cakes, biscuits and sweet offerings. Their comments coupled with the influx of much appreciated requests for sweet recipes received from readers from all walks of life, cultures and generations inspired me to start writing this book a few months later, following the launch of Spice'n' Easy.

Sweets, desserts and impressive baking have long been established in the Asian, Mediterranean and Middle Eastern culture although over the years, outside influences have added new ideas to this vast selection of regional specialities. Most of us second generation British Asians having lived here for the majority of our lives have merged the techniques and styles mixing East with the West quite successfully.

Although the basic principles remain the same, the adaptation and acceptance of new ideas and ingredients brought back from ones travels or via another channel, can only enhance the already delicious selection that one has to offer. We may use exotic ingredients or fruits such as saffron in cakes or papaya in biscuits, but the methods are similar. Surround yourself with these tropical and exotic temptations and utilise their sweet simplicity creating something sensational. It is natural to cling to familiar foods, but inquisitiveness is the key and enthusiasm is the strength. The baking in this book is a compilation of tried, tested, tasted and approved recipes with the inclusion of foreign influences and ingredients.

Baking and serving an assortment of biscuits, cakes, sweets and desserts with an unforced natural blending of ingredients and techniques can only give a deep sense of achievement and immense pleasure. Appreciate the quality of natural home prepared foods where there is nothing pretentious about using the freshest ingredients.

Who can resist freshly baked cakes or fresh home-made biscuits, with the irresistible aroma escaping around the kitchen and house?

Balance the modern preference for lighter cakes and desserts against the inexcusable weakness for richer concoctions. Sweet 'n' Easy provides the reader with a platform for reliable recipes that include a balance of classic and contemporary, simple yet elaborate.

My favourite recipes are passion fruit biscuits, lemon syrup cake, date helawi, saffron buns and walnut wonders. The difference in the size of eggs or the grade of flour may effect the end result, meticulous care should be taken for every small detail. Make your own adjustments to suit your individual tastes. I have always believed that cooking and baking is an art to be enjoyed, so I encourage you to explore your hidden capabilities and talents by exposing them to their full potential.

Use this approach to utilise your time and effort by producing exciting results. Don't be afraid to add or substitute matching ingredients to suit your individual taste. Use your common sense and talent and above all don't abandon your judgement and initiative.

Basic techniques were taught to me by my late mother and elder sisters yet I feel certain that the driving force behind all of us was the genuine interest in good cooking and baking from my late father who treated this subject with a great deal of reverence and respect. To this strong platform to which I am eternally indebted, I added my own personal enthusiasm, learning, experimenting, creating and adapting. Years later my experiences were again strengthened with some input from my parents in law. I was delighted to recognise that this natural streak and hereditary interest had rubbed off onto Rizwaan and Junaid, as we collectively study and observe the local foods and the culture of people we meet on our travels.

It wasn't surprising that by the time I completed this book, my oven had broken down completely with the heavy load and usage it had sustained during those past experimental months.

Sweet 'n' Easy emerged out of my own efforts to blend the East with the West and I hope and believe that you will agree that the richness in blending both these cultures more than compensates for any loss in our own traditional ways. The simple message to my readers is to discover, create and enjoy a happy journey throughout this book.

Because I want you to enjoy reading the book equally as much as tasting the recipes, I have included some light hearted jokes, stories and background information. Overall I have endeavoured to fulfil my aim to accentuate the best from the East and the West and to assist you in enjoying both.
Best Wishes

Hajra Makda

Heating the oven

Pre heat the oven before starting the preparation. This is so that the oven temperature is reached just as the cakes or biscuits are ready to be baked.

How to test cakes

Oven temperatures and cooking times give a reasonable indication, but you can follow basic rules as a guide.

The top of the cake should be springy to the touch, and should rise again leaving no impression behind.

In fruit cakes a continuous sizzling sound indicates that more cooking is required.

A warmed skewer, not a knife, can be inserted in the cake, when removed should come out clean. If not, continue cooking for a while longer.

How to test biscuits

Check the biscuits just before the suggested cooking times have ended.

Observe the colour and touch the cookies gently to see if they are soggy. Different biscuits have different ways of telling you they are ready.

Some will have stayed lightly golden at the top but have browned underneath when picked up.

Follow the individual instructions. Some biscuits need to be removed immediately from the tray whilst others need to rest a couple of minutes before lifting off.

Frosted Fruits and Flowers

Frosted fruits and flowers, make a pretty decoration, dressing up a simple and plain cake making it look elegant and exquisite.

Simple to make, but be sure to only select firm undamaged fruits, and dainty flowers and leaves. Whisk one egg white with 2 teaspoons of cold water.

When it's light and frothy, use a small brush to paint the flowers or fruits individually and then dip in caster sugar.

Shake of any excess and leave to dry on greaseproof paper for almost 24 hours.

Ingredients

Agar Agar is known as Ghas in gujerati and is made from reddish sea weed. It is dried and washed, pounded and dried again before being bleached in the heat of the sun. It is then boiled for almost 24 hours and filtered then cooled.

The gelatinous gel which forms is then rolled thinly into sheets and these are again sun bleached and dried.

Agar agar carries no odour or taste but swells when soaked in cold water. When warmed it will dissolve into a slimy liquid which sets when cooled. It carried almost triples the strength of gelatine and can be used in the powdered form also. Principally used as a setting agent in desserts, ice creams and sauces.

Almonds are the seeds of a tree belonging to the peach family, mostly grown in hot countries such as Sicily, Spain and California. Almonds are frequently used in desserts and in baking. They can be in the form of ground, flaked or powder.

Angelica stalks are in the crystallised or preserved form. Often used for their colour and aroma, angelica is incorporated into cakes, biscuits, puddings and other sweet recipes. Mostly used as a decoration, green in colour and co ordinates well with red cherries.

Arrowroot is a very fine white powder with no flavour. It is used as a thickener in sauces and as a glace where a clear sheen is required. The name arrow root comes from the original use of the powder by American Indians to cure injuries from arrows.

Baking Powder is a combination of two substances and is included in almost every recipe as it gives a lift when baking. It is produced by combining a ratio of one part bicarbonate of soda, and two parts cream of tarter. It is effected by heat and moisture and reacts to produce carbon dioxide gas, which is trapped within the protein structure of the product which is being baked.

Baking Soda is the American equivalent of baking powder, and is the combination of cream of tarter and bicarbonate of soda.

Bicarbonate of Soda is also known in some countries as baking soda. It is usually used as a raising agent for cakes, pastries and breads.

Brazil Nuts are more commonly used in baking now. So called because they are native to Brazil and the Amazon region. Growing inside almost triangular shaped hard shells, which are the seeds of a large fruit. Brazil nuts carry an amazing source of oil. Used whole, chopped or ground.

Butter – Salted or Unsalted is mostly the main ingredient in cakes, biscuits and pastries. Butter has a low melting point and is an invaluable dairy product.

Butter can occasionally be substituted with margarine but is really in a class of its own, imparting a richer and distinct flavour. with a lighter texture. Butter was thought to have been discovered by mistake by the Nomads. They had collected the milk from their goat and cattle and had then separated the cream with the milk, and somehow churned the cream continuously and discovered butter. Most ordinary butters are made up of 80% milk fat and around 16% water with about 3% salt and 2% of non milk solids.

Butter Milk is the liquid which is left behind when the milk has turned to butter.

Caramelisation occurs when fructose, maltase or dextrose is heated to beyond 170° C or 340°F. Then it becomes caramel and undergoes a rapid colour change, turning into an amber brown.

Caster Sugar is a finely ground sugar that is used extensively in baking, for the reason that it dissolves quickly when creamed with butter.

Cinnamon is the thinly rolled inner bark of an evergreen tree. Used extensively as a flavouring for sweet as well as savoury dishes. Commonly used for medicinal purposes too, acting as a digestive and a stimulant, and gentle on the stomach calming it.

Citrus fruits are used often in baking. When using the rind of any citrus fruit, grate it lightly. The white pith imparts a bitter flavour. If only a few drops of the citrus fruit is needed, then pierce the fruit with a fork and squeeze out the juice. Citrus fruits yield more juice if put in a microwave for 30 seconds on high power before squeezing.

Clarified Butter – Ghee is mostly used in Indian cuisine. This is simply butter which has had the water and non fat milk solids removed by rapid boiling.

Melt the butter slowly in a large saucepan. When a froth forms at the surface, use a ladle and scoop away the scum. Into a fresh bowl, ladle the pure golden remaining liquid. The white liquid should have settled to the base. The golden liquid is the clarified butter or ghee which will set. Nowadays it is convenient to purchase a well branded commercially made tin of ghee.

Cocoa Butter is a natural fat derived from the pressing of cocoa beans when producing cocoa mass or cocoa butter. It's a creamy yellow colour when solidified.

Cocoa Powder is used in baking, pastries, biscuits and icings. On its own it's quite bitter. Raw cocoa is often dusted onto the top of cakes and desserts.

Condensed Milk is a very sweet milk sold in tins. It was used widely in England during the war time as it kept well and was substituted for fresh milk. Today it has earned its place in sweet confectionery and pastry making and more often in desserts.

Corn Flour – or Corn Starch is a white powder that is finer then flour. It is extracted from the starch of either wheat or corn, it contains no gluten at all.

Giving shortness to cakes and biscuits making them lighter when a few spoons are substituted for the flour.

Cream is made of many fat particles suspended in water, and when this is churned these globules link together to produce butter.

Cream of Tartar is a fine white powder, which collects in the bottom of casks, in which grapes have fermented. It is refined and sold either by itself or as an ingredient in the raising agent called baking powder.

Dark Brown Soft Sugar is used where rich colour and flavour is required.

Demerara Sugar is a coarse crystal sugar and as the natural colouring of the raw sugar has not been removed, it retains its light brown colour.

Double Cream is a thick cream which has a fat content of around 48%. Used for decorating cakes and in desserts.

Dried Fruits which is sold loosely from a reputable health shop tend to be the freshest due to their large turnover. They are most likely to be fresher then the packaged ones. Store in appropriate containers in a cold dark place. To rehydrate fruit seep in hot water for about half an hour.

Eggs that are used in this book and in the recipes are large in size. It is important to use the correct size or the mixture will be either too dry or wet. Eggs are much easier to separate when they are cold and are best used at room temperature as very cold eggs tend to curdle the mixture. You can bring them to room temperature by placing in a warm bowl for a few minutes. Egg whites should always be whisked at room temperature, in a dry and grease free bowl to ensure that they are whisked to their maximum volume.

Essences are made by extracting the flavour from the food by a natural process.

Fats and Oils are some times replaceable. Butter and block margarine are interchangeable in baking. Butter gives a richer flavour and extends the life of cakes keeping them fresher. If the butter is too hard then beat alone, until softened or use the microwave to soften. Vegetable oils can be used in specially proportioned recipes.

Fennel has excellent qualities and a very soothing effect if induced in hot water and taken as a drink, or if boiled in milk and sweetened with honey. Drunk warm it can be relaxing as well as encouraging a good nights sleep.

Figs should not be too sticky when bought. The compressed blocks would benefit from soaking before use.

Flavourings are synthetic and tend to be cheaper. Both essences and flavourings have very strong flavours and usually only a few drops are required in a recipe.

Flours are included in most of the recipes, either plain or self raising.
   Always making a habit to sift the flour once or twice is even better. The reason why the amount of liquid required to bind the ingredients together can alter slightly is due to the grade in the flour. Self raising flour already contains raising agents and so baking powder must only be used when specified.

Glucose is the thick clear form of sugar. This is produced by the break down of starch cells which have been treated with acids and enzymes, then fermented to form sugars.

Golden Syrup is used to make sauces for rich puddings and to flavour biscuits, cakes and fillings. Known sometimes as light treacle, golden in colour and is quite thick.

Hazel Nuts are the fruit of the Hazel bush. They are round, brown skinned hard nuts with cream coloured insides. Rich with oil and excellent nutritional values. First discovered and enjoyed by the Chinese and later spreading to Europe and other parts of the world. Usually roasted to bring out a fuller flavour then ground for use in cakes and biscuits particularly.

Helwa is a confection made in many countries, usually from sugar, ghee or butter and with some flour and nuts etc. The flavourings and additions differ from country to country. Traditionally Helwa is flavoured with rose water and a little saffron, cinnamon and cardammon.

Honey is used in some recipes. It absorbs and retains moisture and keeps the products fresh.

Icing Sugar is simply a powdered form of sugar which has been ground to a dust and which dissolves instantly. It is included in icings in used mainly for cakes and pastries. Icing sugar gives a softer finish when dusted over the top of cakes and biscuits.

Light Brown Sugar can be used to replace caster sugar where more colour and flavour can be achieved.

Macadamia Nuts are a native Australian nut. Dr John Macadam discovered them in the native Queensland rainforest in 1857. The nuts are encased within a firm shell and are prized in cooking for their smooth buttery flavour. They are also pressed for their oil. Now widely produced in hot climates such as Malawi and the Hawaiian Islands.

Oatmeal is produced by removing the husks and separating the grain and shaft from the oats. The oats are then ground to a powder which can vary from coarse to fine in texture. Oatmeal is hulled oats, ground into four grades. Coarse, medium, fine and pin head.

Orange Flower Water is a distilled liquid from the orange blossom of the Seville orange tree. Orange flower water has been used for centuries in the manufacture of many sweet dishes as well as baking. Particularly in countries such as Turkey, Iran and some parts of Africa.

Peanuts have known to be in existent for thousands of years. They are natives to South America but spread to South Africa and around the world.

Plain Flour can be used with a raising agent which can be varied to suit individual recipes.

Praline is the name given to crushed caramelised almonds. Useful in adding texture and flavour to butter cream and cake fillings, or as a decoration.

Rind is the outer skin of citrus fruits and grated finely for flavouring for use in baking. It can even be cut into strips for crystallising and garnishing. It contains essentials oils which can also be removed by rubbing the rind with sugar cubes.

Rose Water is a highly fragrant rose flavoured water. It is used widely in Middle Eastern and Asian sweets and desserts.

Salted Butter is used in the production of large cakes and pastries when the main flavour is not that of the butter and where the salt taste will not overpower. Instead it will simply harmonise with the other flavours present. Salt added to butter can also pro-long the life of the product.

Self Raising Flour is popular because it eliminates errors. The raising agents are already evenly blended within the flour.

Single Cream is a thinner cream, excellent for pouring and cooking when more creaminess is required then milk. It has only the minimum of 18% fat.

Soured Cream is a versatile product made with fresh single cream, that has been soured by adding a natural culture similar to that used in yoghurt. It is distinctive and unique as a dairy product.

Sugar Thermometer is a thermometer which is marked with the temperatures at which changes occur in sugar.

Tapioca is a form of starch which is extracted from the roots of the cassava plant. This is a small shrub of which there are some 2000 varieties. Tapioca is used as a thickener in puddings. It swells and becomes very clear when boiled in a liquid, making it perfect to use in milk and milk based puddings or thickened desserts. It is most commonly sold in the pearl form.

Treacle is a sweet and dark by product of the sugar refining process. Treacle is the liquid which remains after processing has taken place. It is also known as golden syrup, but this the lighter form of treacle. Darker treacle is sweeter with a more intense flavour and colour. Both are used in exactly the same way to give flavour and colour especially in cakes and confectionery.

Unsalted Butter is used in recipes where the flavour of butter is required without a salty taste added. Usually in sweet recipes such as hazel nut whirls, nutty slices and apricot treats.

Vanilla was introduced in Europe when discovered in Mexico where the Aztecs had been using vanilla pods in the production of chocolate.

Vanilla Essence is made by soaking the pods in pure alcohol to extract the flavouring. Brown colouring is added to give the essence an attractive appearance.
  The alcohol is cleverly disguised in products and in chemical terms is better known as 'propylene glycol' or as 'as ethanol alcohol.' I don't want to start a national panic for those of us who don't consume alcohol in any form, but vanilla essence and flavouring does contain minute amounts of alcohol. I cross checked with various companies, pharmacists and manufacturers who confirmed this. I was surprised myself having used this product for years but if you are worried you may want to check yourself. Vanilla pods are not expensive and last a good few months.

Vanilla Sugar, is sugar in which a vanilla pod has been stored so that it's flavour permeates the sugar. Alternatively vanillin can be added to the sugar and is used in recipes in the same way as normal caster sugar. This imparts a lovely and stronger flavour and makes the baking just a little bit special. Use to replace vanilla essence and flavouring in all recipes if desired.

Vanilla Pods are a fruit of a Mexican climbing orchid and grow 12-20 cm in length. It is picked while still in its green stage and cured and dried until black and aromatic. Once dried the pods must be kept in air tight jars to retain their flavours.

   The pods are often used in sauces and cremes by boiling with milk and cream and then being allowed to infuse for some time. You can remove and wash for reusing. Vanillin is a synthetic flavour which is subtler then the natural product.

Whipping Cream is a lighter version of double cream, with at least 35% fat content and whips easily without the richness. Excellent as a pouring cream or for swirling on desserts.

Wholemeal or Whole Wheat is a flour which is made up from the whole grain of wheat. It has nothing removed after the milling process. The dough's or batters with this added tend to soak up more liquid and therefore require more water.

Basic Icings

Butter Icing
The silky smoothness and creamy rich flavour of this cream is very popular with most people.

   Like most icings you can make your own flavours with appropriate colours, and these can then be used to sandwich cakes or fill swiss rolls or even just for decorating the top of the cake.

   Spread onto a cake and swirl with a fork or pipe out some elaborate designs. Butter icing really gives a delicious and attractive finish.

   The following quantity can make enough to cover a round 20 cm- 8 inch cake.

Ingredients
85 g - 3 oz softened butter
225 g - 8 oz icing sugar
1 tsp vanilla essence
2-3 tsp milk

Method
In a mixing bowl, put the butter, sugar, vanilla and 1 tsp of milk.

   Beat well with a wooden spoon or an electric mixer adding more milk if required to make light and fluffy consistency. Use as required.

Suggested flavourings.
Chocolate: Blend 1 tbsp cocoa with 1 tbsp boiling water. Omit the milk and allow to cool before icing.
Coffee: Blend 2 tsp instant coffee with 1 tbsp boiling water. Cool before beating into the icing. Omit the milk.

Fudge Frosting
This delicious frosting is rich, dark and very tempting.

   Easily impress your guests by transforming a simple sponge or Madeira cake into something very special.

   Pipe the frosting on the cake or simply swirl and decorate with your own style.

   The following recipe is enough for a 23 cm - 9 inch cake.

Ingredients
55 g - 2 oz plain chocolate
225 g - 8 oz icing sugar
55 g - 2 oz butter
3 tbsp single cream or milk
1 tsp vanilla essence

Method
Break the chocolate into small pieces. In a heavy saucepan mix the chocolate, icing sugar, butter, milk and vanilla essence together. Stir very slowly over the lowest heat until the butter and chocolate have melted. Remove from the heat and continue to stir until evenly blended.

Beat the icing frequently as it cools until it thickens sufficiently for spreading or piping. Once it has reached the right consistency use quickly to avoid setting.

Glace Icing

Glace icing is made in a matter of minutes, and can have many varied flavours. Just a few drops of flavouring or colouring can transform the icing for cakes and biscuits making them more appealing. The following quantity can make enough to cover a round 20 cm - 8 inch cake.

Ingredients
225 g - 8 oz icing sugar
2-3 tbsp warm water or fruit juice
Food colouring

Method
Sift the icing sugar into a bowl. Then using a wooden spoon, gradually stir in enough water until it has reached the consistency of thick cream.

Beat well until the icing is smooth. It should be thick enough to coat the back of a spoon. If it has become runny then mix in some more sifted icing sugar.

Apricot Glace

Ingredients
225 g - 8 oz apricot jam
3 tbsp water
2 tsp lemon juice

Place all the ingredients in a saucepan and stir until thoroughly blended.

Cook over a high heat for 5 minutes or in a microwave at high power.

Force through a wire strainer and then brush over the cake whilst still warm. Allow to cool before the icing is applied.

Arrow Root Glace

Ingredients
3 tbsp arrow root powder
22 fl oz fruit juice
or cordial syrup

Method
Mix the arrow root with a little of the juice to make a smooth paste. Place remaining liquid in a saucepan and slowly bring to the boil.

When boiling, pour the liquid over the arrow root mixture and stir until both are well combined.

Return to the saucepan and allow to heat until the mixture thickens and clears.

Strain if necessary and use immediately whilst still warm for glazing.

If the syrup is not sweet enough you may need to add a little sugar to the unboiled syrup. This can be adapted to suit whatever you are glacing, with assorted flavourings and colouring.

Chocolate Glace

Ingredients
25 g - 1 oz plain chocolate
1 tbsp water
115 g - 4 oz sifted icing sugar.

Method
Melt the chocolate and water together in a small pan and then leave to cool slightly. Add the icing sugar and beat until smooth and spreadable.

Light Cream

If you don't like the heavy and very sweet icings on cake. Try this one, it is simple to make and extremely light and creamy.

Ingredients
125 g - 5 oz soft butter
115 g - 4 oz caster sugar
4 tbsp boiling water
4 tbsp cold milk or cream
Few drops vanilla essence

Method
Cream the butter and sugar thoroughly for about 20 minutes, then gradually add the boiling water to it.

Continue beating for another 12 minutes then add the milk when no trace of the sugar remains. Beat for another 10 minutes until light and fluffy then add the essence for a few minutes longer. The cream should be ready to spread onto the cakes now.

Marzipan

Marzipan has been a popular icing for centuries. With it's smooth, pliable texture it is popular for celebration cakes, such as birthday's or weddings.

Marzipan can be cut out into individual shapes for making decorations.

Once the marzipan has been applied, leave to dry for almost 12 hours before icing.

It is possible to make your own marzipan but since it contains uncooked eggs you may have cause for concern.

It is recommended then that you buy the ready made one which comes in a variety of colours and is of exceptionally good quality.

Sugar Paste Icing

Sugar paste icing has opened up a whole new concept to cake decorating.

Very easy to use, pliable and can be coloured and moulded and shaped in any form or shape.

Commercially made sugar paste icing doesn't contain raw eggs, as the home made one does.

It is often referred to as 'easy roll,' or 'ready to roll icing.'

Colourings

Food colourings are available in almost any shade and have opened endless opportunities for the enthusiastic decorator.

Liquid colours are suitable for marzipan, butter icing and sugar paste icing. Only a few drops are needed to tint the icing, too many and the icing will soften.

For stronger or more vibrant colours it is recommended that you use the powders available from most food stores.

These are concentrated and you only need the slightest to create an attractive effect that won't alter the consistency of the icing.

When choosing colours and flavourings, make sure they are harmonious with the taste of the cake and that the design compliments the flavour.

Oven Temperatures

275°F	140°C	Gas Mark 1
300°F	150°C	Gas Mark 2
325°F	160°C	Gas Mark 3
350°F	180°C	Gas Mark 4
375°F	190°C	Gas Mark 5
400°F	200°C	Gas Mark 6
425°F	220°C	Gas Mark 7
450°F	230°C	Gas Mark 8
475°F	240°C	Gas Mark 9
500°F	250°C	Gas Mark 10

Cakes & Buns

Golden *Crunch Cake p19*

Carrot *Cake*

This cake remains moist and light for a few days and is delicious with an optional frosting.

Ingredients

225 g – 8 oz butter
225 g – 8 oz light brown soft sugar
4 eggs, separated
Finely grated rind of 1/2 an orange
1 tbsp lemon juice
175 g – 6 oz self raising flour
1 tsp baking powder
55 g – 2 oz ground almonds
115 g – 4 oz chopped walnuts
350 g – 12 oz grated carrots

Method

350˚F – 180˚C - Gas Mark 4

Cream the butter and sugar in a bowl until light and fluffy. Beat in the egg yolks and then stir in the orange rind and the lemon juice.

Sift in the flour and the baking powder, then stir in the almonds and walnuts.

In a glass bowl which is completely dry, whisk the egg whites until stiff.

Fold the carrots into the cake mixture then pour into a greased 20 cm - 8" cake tin.

Bake in a pre heated oven for about 1.5 hours. If it has browned before that time, then cover with foil or brown paper until the cooking time is over.

Leave to cool in the tin for about 10 minutes then turn out onto a cooling tray.

You may wish to use an icing such as Mock Icing to cover the cake.

Cinnamon *Cakes*

These cakes are sprinkled with sugar and cinnamon and are very simple to make.

Ingredients

55 g – 2 oz butter
2 tbsp vegetable oil
225 g – 8 oz sugar
1 egg
225 g – 8 oz self raising flour
1.5 tsp baking powder
1/2 tsp salt
1/2 tsp cinnamon powder
4 fl oz milk

Topping
1 tsp powdered cinnamon
1 tsp caster sugar
55 g – 2 oz melted butter

Method

350˚F – 180˚C - Gas Mark 4

In a mixing bowl beat the 55 g - 2 oz butter and the oil with half of the sugar.

Into this mixture, beat the eggs until light and creamy, then whisk in the milk.

Sift the flour, baking powder, salt, cinnamon powder and fold all together with a metal spoon.

Spoon this mixture into twelve cake cases and bake for 25 minutes. After this time the cakes should be lightly golden.

Take out from the oven and immediately brush the melted butter over them. Sprinkle the powdered cinnamon, and caster sugar for that extra flavour.

Passion *Fruit Cake*

This cake has layers of exotic fruit filling, ideal for a summer buffet. It takes a little longer to make but is equally rewarding.

Ingredients
4 eggs, separated
115 g – 4 oz caster sugar
115 g – 4 oz self raising flour
Pinch of salt
25 g – 1 oz unsalted butter, melted

Cream
350 g – 12 oz fromage blanc
5 tbsp thick natural yoghurt
4 drops of orange flower water
3 tsp icing sugar
5 ripe passion fruits, halved

Decoration
150 – 5 fl oz double cream-lightly whipped
115 g – 4 oz chopped pistachio nuts
Shelled pistachio nuts and almonds

Method
350°F – 180°C - Gas Mark 4

Whisk the egg yolks and sugar together in a bowl. When thick and pale sift the flour and salt into the bowl then fold in lightly. Whisk the egg whites until stiff but not dry. Lightly fold into the yolk mixture.

Trickle the butter over and carefully fold in. Prepare a baking tin by greasing a 23 cm or 9" loose based cake tin. Line the base with greaseproof paper.

Bake in a pre heated oven for almost 30 minutes, until well risen.

Leave to cool slightly in the tin before turning out onto a cooling tray.

Remove the lining paper and leave to cool completely.

To make the cream, mix together the fromage blanc, yoghurt, orange flower water and the icing sugar together in a bowl. Stir in the passion fruit flesh.

Cut the cake into three equal layers. Spread 1/3rd of the cream over the bottom layer, place the 2nd layer over the top and cover spread the cream again. Then gently place the top of the cake and then cream again.

For the decoration, you can pipe some rosettes over the top of the cake and spread the remaining cream around the sides.

Finish the decoration by coating the sides with the chopped nuts.

Orange flower water is a transparent, distilled liquid from the concentrated essence of the orange blossom of the Seville orange tree. Purified water is than added to dilute it. Orange flower water has been used for centuries in the manufacture of many sweet dishes as well as baking, confectionery and desserts. Particularly in countries such as Turkey, Iran and some parts of Africa.

Apricot & Cherry Muffins

Increasingly popular nowadays and quick to make.

Ingredients

1 medium sized orange
200 g – 7 oz plain brown flour
115 g – 4 oz soft light brown sugar
25 g – 1 oz wheatgerm
1 tsp baking powder
1 tsp bicarbonate of soda
4 tbsp orange juice
55 g – 2 oz vegetable margarine
1 egg
55 g – 2 oz red cherries
55 g – 2 oz dried apricots

Method

400 °F – 200 °C - Gas Mark 6

Take the orange and grate the rind into a bowl. Add the sifted flour, sugar, wheat germ, baking powder and the soda. Rub the sugar into the mixture until it resembles fine breadcrumbs.

Peel the orange and separate into segments, then take the pips out.

In a blender pour in the juice, add the orange, margarine, egg, cherries and apricots and blend for a couple of minutes. Pour this onto the dry mixture and stir carefully, until everything is just mixed. Arrange muffin cases in a 12 hole bun tin and spoon this mixture into the cases.

Bake in the centre of a pre heated oven for almost 20 minutes or until cooked.

Don't allow the oven to be opened during this process.

When baked lift out onto a cooling tray.

Seed Cake

Take a glance at the ingredients list and surprise yourself with the finished product.

Ingredients

115 g – 4 oz marg
115 g – 4 oz caster sugar
2 large eggs
150 g – 5 oz self raising flour
55 g – 2 oz ground almonds
2 tsp caraway seeds
1 tsp fennel seeds
2 tbsp brown sugar
1 tbsp almond flakes

Method

350 °F – 180 °C - Gas mark 4

Cream the marg and sugar with an electric mixer until very light and fluffy. Beat the eggs separately and gradually beat into the mixture.

When all the eggs have been incorporated, taking a metal spoon gently fold in the ground almonds, caraway seeds, fennel seeds and the sifted flour.

Add enough cold milk to give a dropping consistency.

Grease a 7"-18 cm round tin and line with greaseproof paper.

Spoon in the mixture then level out the surface with a spatula and sprinkle the demerara sugar and crushed almonds.

Bake in the centre of a pre heated oven. The cake should be baked in an hour and will have begun to shrink away.

Cool in the tin for almost ten minutes then turn out onto a wire tray to cool completely.

Fennel itself has a lot of qualities and contains soothing properties if induced in hot water and taken as a drink. Try boiling it in milk and sweeten with honey. Drinking this warm can be relaxing as well as encouraging a good nights sleep. Fennel is frequently eaten after meals for it's digestive properties.

Apricot & *Cherry Muffins*

Date *Muffins*

Amazingly succulent and moist muffins with the additions of dates.

Ingredients

1 medium sized orange
200 g – 7 oz plain brown flour
115 g – 4 oz soft light brown sugar
25 g – 1 oz wheatgerm
1 tsp baking powder
1 tsp bicarbonate of soda
4 tbsp orange juice
55 g – 2 oz vegetable margarine
1 egg
85 g – 3 oz chopped dates

Method

400°F – 200°C - Gas Mark 6

Take the orange and grate the rind into a bowl. Add the sifted flour, sugar, wheat germ, baking powder and the soda. Rub the sugar into the mixture until it resembles fine breadcrumbs.

Peel the orange and separate into segments, then take the pips out.

In a blender pour in the juice, add the orange, margarine, egg and dates and blend for 7-8 minutes. Pour this onto the dry mixture and stir carefully, until everything is just mixed. Grease a 12 hole, bun tin with melted margarine and spoon this mixture carefully into the tin.

Bake in the centre of a pre heated oven for almost 20 minutes or until cooked.

Don't allow the oven to be opened during this process.

When baked lift the edges carefully with a sharp knife and cool on a tray.

Eat warm drizzled with honey if you like.

Featherlight *Sponge*

Like its namesake, a very light cake with the addition of corn flour.

Ingredients

150 g – 5 oz plain flour
55 g – 2 oz corn flour
2 tsp baking powder
1/2 tsp salt
150 g – 5 oz caster sugar
2 eggs, separated
3.5 fl oz corn oil
3.5 fl oz water

Method

375°F – 190°C - Gas Mark 5

Sift all the dry ingredients twice. In a separate bowl beat the egg yolks well until light and then beat again with the corn oil and water. Stir this liquid into the dry mixture then beat well to form a batter like mixture. Whisk the egg whites stiffly before very lightly folding into the mixture.

Prepare 2 tins by lining with lightly greased, paper.

Bake in a pre heated oven for around 25 minutes.

When cooled sandwich together with red jam and fresh cream.

Two large friends stopped at a coffee house intrigued by a sign which offered fat free cakes.

They had been dieting for weeks and the need to eat the cakes was so overwhelming.

Rather pleased with themselves at spotting this place they wondered whether to ask for the recipe so they could indulge in the cakes at home on a regular basis.

Giving her a large tip they plucked up enough courage to ask the waitress who served them.

"Yes sure, just a minute, I'll write it down."

After a few minutes the two friends glanced down the list of ingredients and asked in dismay, "Hey, I thought the cakes we ate were fat free? There's oil in here."

"Yes, course they're fat free," she replied innocently. "We only charge for the service and the other ingredients, but the oil is free."

Ginger *Cake*

This delicious cake really contains natural and warming ingredients, just right for a cold winters day.

Ingredients

225 g – 8 oz treacle
85 g – 3 oz sugar
225 g – 8 oz flour
1 tsp bicarbonate of soda
3 tsp ground ginger
115 g – 4 oz butter
225 g – 8 oz sultanas
1 egg
2 tbsp lemon juice
150 ml – 1/4 pt milk

Method

325°F – 170°C - Gas Mark 3

Warm the treacle and sugar gently until it has liquidified and the sugar has dissolved, then cool. In the meantime sift the flour and soda together adding the ground ginger.

Rub in the butter and mix in the raisins. Make a well in the centre of the dry ingredients and add the cooled liquid, egg, lemon juice and milk.

Beat well together until thoroughly mixed.

Pour into a lightly greased 7" cake tin and bake in a pre heated oven.

Test with a skewer and when cooked cool for 15 minutes before turning out onto a wire tray.

Golden *Crunch Cake*

This cake is so simple to make and has a wonderful crunchy topping.

Ingredients

175 g – 6 oz butter
175 g – 6 oz caster sugar
4 eggs
55 g – 2 oz icing sugar
225 g – 8 oz self raising flour
2 tbsp milk
55 g – 2 oz desiccated coconut

Method

325°F – 160°C - Gas Mark 3

Cream together the butter and sugar with an electric mixer.

Take two of the eggs and separate the yolks from the whites. Beat together the yolks and the other two eggs until frothy and light. Take two tbsp of flour and beat well with the eggs.

Gradually add to the creamy mixture.

Fold in the remaining flour with a metal spoon and spread into two greased 6" tins.

Wash and dry the whisk, then beat the egg whites till very stiff.

Add the icing sugar to this and fold in the coconut.

Pile this meringue onto the mixture and bake in a preheated oven.

After almost 50 minutes, the cakes should be ready. Allow a few minutes in the tins then transfer onto a cooling tray.

Bill and Ben, the children of two close friends were playing together during afternoon tea. Because they were so well behaved they were given permission to eat the last two slices of the delicious cake.

Bill quickly takes the biggest one at which Ben complains bitterly. "Hey! That's not fair that's bad manners!"

Bill asks with a triumphant smile "Well, what would YOU have done?"

Ben immediately replies with a flicker of hope. "Of course I would've taken the smaller one and left YOU the larger slice!"

Bill laughed and replied before he took a large bite of the cake, "Well what's the problem then you've got the smaller one."

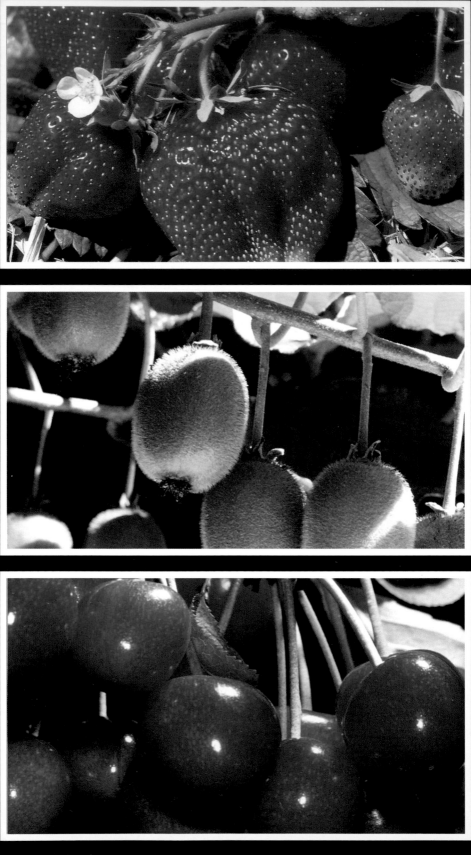

Some *of the fruits used in my recipes*

Coffee *Cakes*

Sweet little cakes with a hint of coffee. Delicious aroma escapes from the oven when baking.

Ingredients
175 g – 6 oz margarine
175 g –- 6 oz caster sugar
2 eggs
2 tbsp warm water
2 tbsp coffee
225 g – 8 oz self raising flour

Method
375˚F – 190˚C - Gas Mark 5

In a mixing bowl, beat together the margarine and sugar.

Beat the eggs separately and add a little at a time to the creamy mixture.

Dissolve the coffee in the warm water and add this to the mixture.

Using a metal spoon fold in the sifted flour and mix gently but well together.

Fill a baking sheet with cake cases and drop a tablespoon of the mixture in each case.

Bake in a pre heated oven until well risen and then cool on a cooling tray.

Coffee is one of the most widely known and used commodities in the world today. According to legend in around 1000 AD, a shepherd in Ethiopia noticed that his flocks of goats became more energetic and playful after being fed on the local plants. He sampled a little of what they'd eaten and really enjoyed the taste of the coffee bean. He then took the beans to a local monastery where the monks produced a drink by roasting the seeds, crushing them and adding boiling water. They all enjoyed it immensely and were surprised to find that it even kept them awake during their prayers.

However, coffee never really became popular until the 16th century when coffee houses began opening throughout European countries. They soon become fashionable and said something about one's social status. This plant is grown in countries such as Brazil, Columbia and Zimbabwe as well as Malawi and other African countries. Coffee takes an average of four years for the shoots to produce the beans which are contained within the red cherry like fruit.

Date *Cakes*

Middle Eastern cakes with the addition of honey to retain moistness.

Ingredients
175 g – 6 oz butter
4 tbsp light brown sugar
4 fl oz clear honey
4 lightly beaten eggs
350 g – 12 oz self raising flour
2 tsp mixed spice
4 - 6 fl oz milk
115 g – 4 oz dates finely chopped

Method
400˚F – 200˚C - Gas Mark 6

Beat the butter, sugar and honey together in a mixing bowl. Gradually add the beaten eggs beating all the time.

Add 225 g - 8 oz of sifted flour and the mixed spice and fold in gently with a metal spoon.

Add sufficient milk to give a dropping consistency.

In a small, separate bowl sprinkle the 115 g - 4 oz of remaining flour and rub over the chopped dates. This is to prevent the dates from sinking as they cook.

Add to the batter and fold in.

Spoon into 24 cake cases and cook for 20 minutes or until golden and springy to the touch.

Hazelnut *Cake*

Delicious cake cut into squares and with a very unusual topping.

Ingredients

55 g – 2 oz margarine
85 g – 3 oz soft light brown sugar
2 eggs, separated
Juice and rind of 2 oranges
150 g – 5 oz plain brown flour
1 tsp baking powder
85 g – 3 oz ground hazelnuts
1 piece of Shredded Wheat biscuit

Topping
3 tbsp clear honey
2 tbsp orange juice
1 piece of shredded wheat, crumbled
25 g – 1 oz toasted nuts

Method
350°F – 180°C - Gas Mark 4

Cream the margarine and sugar together until light and fluffy. Add the separated egg yolks one at a time. Then add the flour and baking powder gradually alternating with the juice of the oranges. Crumble the shredded wheat and add this to the mixture. Finally whisk the egg whites until stiff, and fold into the cake mixture using a large metal spoon. Grease a deep 20 cm - 8 inch square tin and bake in the centre of a pre heated oven for almost 40 minutes. By then the cake should have risen well and turned lightly golden.

Remove the cake from the tin and whilst still warm add the topping.

Combine all the ingredients together and pour gently over the cake, with a fork smooth out into the edges. Cut into squares with a sharp knife and serve when cold.

Red *Cherry Cake*

This cake is so called because it contains cherries, which sink during the cooking process forming a moist and juicy layer. Looks and tastes delicious when sliced.

Ingredients

225 g – 8 oz softened butter
225 g – 8 oz caster sugar
4 eggs, lightly whisked
225 g – 8 oz plain flour
1/2 tsp baking powder
225 g – 8 oz glace cherries
115 g – 4 oz ground almonds
Few drops of vanilla essence
2 tbsp demerara sugar
1 tbsp milk

Method
350°F – 180°C - Gas Mark 4

Beat the butter and sugar together until light and fluffy. Beat in the eggs a little at a time then sift in the flour and baking powder together.

Fold this into the creamed mixture lightly with a metal spoon. Add the cherries and the almonds in together and fold lightly into the cake.

Add a few drops of essence and the milk to ease the mixing. Spoon the mixture into a greased 20 cm - 8" tin and level with the back of a spoon.

Sprinkle the demerara sugar and bake for an hour in the centre of the oven.

Cover with foil and continue to cook for a further 30 minutes or until the cake has shrunk away from the sides of the tin.

Cool for almost 10 minutes then continue cooling on a wire rack.

**TIP : If you don't want the cherries to sink, wash the syrup and quarter the cherries. Dry thoroughly and mix in a little flour.

Honey *Cake*

Try this freshly baked warm cake, sliced and spread with butter.

Ingredients

1.5 oz – 1 tsp butter
300 g – 10 oz self raising flour
150 ml – 5 fl oz clear honey
55 g – 2 oz soft brown sugar
70 ml – 2 fl oz milk
3 eggs
1 tsp bicarb of soda
1 tbsp milk
1/2 tsp ground ginger
Pinch of salt
1/2 tsp ground mixed spice
1/2 tsp ground cloves
55 g – 2 oz flaked pistachio nuts

Method

325 °F – 170 °C - Gas Mark 3

Lightly grease a 20 cm - 8" round tin with 1 tsp of butter, then sprinkle the 1 tbsp of flour into the tin and shake out the access flour.

In a saucepan, combine the honey, sugar and remaining butter stirring constantly on a low heat until the sugar and butter have dissolved completely

Remove the pan from the heat and set aside.

In a medium sized mixing bowl, beat together the milk, eggs and the bicarbonate of soda. Sift the remaining ingredients into the large bowl and into the middle pour in the honey, milk and the egg mixture.

Using a metal spoon mix together gently until smooth and creamy.

When all is smooth, pour the batter into the prepared cake tin.

Sprinkle the flaked pistachio over and bake in the centre of a pre heated oven for approximately an hour. Test to see if the cake is cooked then cool slightly in the tin then turn out onto a wire tray. Slice whilst still warm and serve with butter.

A well known senator is in a restaurant when the waiter brings over the rolls, but no butter. "May I have some butter, please?" he asks politely.

The waiter gives a slight nod but ten minutes later, there is still no butter.

Frustrated he calls to the waiter, "May I have some butter, please?" He receives a nod and still no butter appears. By this time he is getting really annoyed.

He walks over to the waiter who is pre occupied with another customer and raises his voice so all the other diners can hear him. "Maybe you don't know who I am," he says. "I'm a Princeton graduate, a Rhodes scholar, I'm currently a United States Senator and Chairman of the International Debt Subcommittee of the Senate Finance Committee." He looks down at the waiter with glee waiting for an answer. "Maybe you don't know who I am," says the waiter. "I'm the guy who's in charge of the butter!"

Lemon *Syrup Cake*

Lemon *Syrup Cake*

A delicious tangy cake with an equally delicious syrup.

Ingredients
200 g – 7 oz plain flour
2 tsp baking powder
200 g – 7 oz caster sugar
4 eggs
150 ml – 5 fl oz sour cream
Grated rind of a large lemon
1 tbsp lemon juice
150 ml – 5 fl oz sunflower oil

Syrup
4 tbsp icing sugar
3 tbsp lemon juice

Method
350˚F – 180˚C - Gas Mark 4

Sieve the flour and the baking powder into a bowl and stir in the sugar.

In a separate bowl whisk the eggs, sour cream, rind and juice all together.

Stir this egg mixture into the flour and mix well until evenly combined.

Pour the mixture into a lightly greased and lined 20 cm - 8" loose bottom round cake tin. Bake for about an hour until well risen and golden brown.

To make the syrup, mix together the ingredients in a small saucepan and stir over a low heat until it just begins to bubble. As soon as the cake comes out of the oven, prick the surface with a fine skewer to make sure that the syrup sinks right into the cake, when poured over the top. Cool the cake completely in it's own tin and allow the syrup to soak in before turning out to serve.

Swiss *Cakes*

These cakes are delicious on their own or they can be dusted with icing sugar.

Ingredients
25 g – 1 oz butter + 2 tsp melted butter
85 g – 3 oz soft brown sugar
1 tsp ground all spice
1/4 tsp ground cinnamon
2 tbsp sultanas or seedless raisins
85 g – 3 oz chopped walnuts
1 egg yolk
2 tbsp milk

Dough
225 g – 8 oz flour
1/2 tsp baking powder
Pinch of salt
1.5 oz butter
4 tbsp milk

Method
400˚F – 200˚C - Gas Mark 6

Make the dough by sifting the flour, baking powder and salt into a mixing bowl.

Cut the butter into small pieces and add to the flour. Using your fingertips rub in the butter using the breadcrumb method.

Beat the egg yolks with the milk and mix just enough into the dry mixture to make a firm dough. Shape the dough into a ball and turn out onto a lightly floured working surface. Knead lightly till smooth. Roll the dough into an oblong, and using a pastry brush, brush the dough with melted butter.

In a small mixing bowl combine the fruit with the walnuts and sugar. Sprinkle this over the dough leaving a margin around the edges.

Roll firmly and tightly like a swiss roll.

Using the pastry brush, brush the roll with the milk mixture.

Cover with foil and place in fridge for an hour. After an hour take out the firm roll and cut into 12 slices.

Arrange on a greased baking sheet and bake in the centre of a pre heated oven. Bake until cooked and the pastries are golden brown. Remove and cool glazing with apricot jam if desired.

Nut *Coated Cake*

This cake is quick to make, the best part of it is in the topping made within minutes.

Ingredients

200 g – 7 oz softened butter
Finely grated zest of one lemon
150 g – 5 oz caster sugar
3 medium sized eggs
85 g – 3 oz sifted, plain flour
150 g – 5 oz sifted, self raising flour

Topping

3 tbsp clear light honey
115 g – 4 oz mixed peel
55 g – 2 oz flaked almonds

Method

350°F – 180°C - Gas Mark 4

Grease a 450 g -1 lb loaf tin and line the base and sides with grease proof paper.

Grease the paper with melted butter or vegetable oil.

In a large mixing bowl, place the butter, lemon zest and sugar in a mixing bowl, then beat until light and fluffy.

Beat in the eggs one at a time until evenly blended.

Sift together the flours then stir into the mixture using a metal spoon.

Transfer the mixture into the loaf tin and then smooth the surface with a table knife dipped in hot water.

Bake in the centre of the oven for 40-45 minutes or until a skewer inserted inside comes out clean.

Leave to rest for 5 minutes then peel off the paper.

Turn out onto a wire tray to cool completely.

To add the finishing touch, place the honey, chopped mixed peel and almonds in a small saucepan and heat gently until the honey melts.

Remove from the heat and stir briefly to coat the peel and the almonds and spread on top of the cake.

Cool completely before serving.

Orange zest is the essential oil extracted from the rind of oranges.

The zest can easily be extracted at home for baking and cooking purposes. Possibly the easiest way to do this is by rubbing a sugar cube over the rind and you will see the cube being soaked up with the oil. Crush the cube and use it when zest is required. Do not confuse zest with rind.

Eggless *Cake*

This fruit cake doesn't contain any eggs. Here the bicarbonate of soda and the vinegar act as raising agents.

Ingredients

225 g – 8 oz butter
450 g – 1 lb plain flour
450 g – 1 lb mixed dried fruit
225 g – 8 oz soft brown sugar
1 tsp bicarbonate of soda
300 ml – 1/2 pt fresh milk
3 tbsp malt vinegar

Method

400°F – 200°C - Gas Mark 6

Rub the butter into the flour until it resembles breadcrumbs, then add the fruit and sugar. Sprinkle the bicarbonate of soda into the milk and add the vinegar. This will begin to froth up and start foaming.

Add it to the other ingredients while it's still foaming and mix well. Turn the mixture into a lightly greased, deep 23 cm - 9" round tin.

Bake at 400°F - 200°C - Mark 6 for 30 minutes. After that time reduce the temperature to 325°F - 170°C - Mark 3 and continue to bake for another 1.5 hours or until firm to the touch.

If the top gets brown before it is cooked then cover with brown paper and continue cooking. Leave to cool in the tin for 30 minutes then turn out onto a wire to cool completely.

Almond *Cake*

The appearance and taste of this cake is so attractive with honey glace dripping naturally down the sides.

Ingredients
115 g – 4 oz butter
85 g – 3 oz caster sugar
2 tbsp clear honey
2 lightly beaten eggs
175 g – 6 oz self raising flour
115 g – 4 oz halved glace cherries
55 g – 2 oz chopped blanched almonds

Glace
1 tbsp clear honey
85 g – 3 oz sieved icing sugar
55 g – 2 oz glace cherries
55 g – 2 oz blanched almonds

Method
350˚F – 180˚C - Gas Mark 4

Cream the butter, sugar and honey together until light and fluffy.

Gradually beat in the eggs, adding 1 tbsp of flour with the last amount.

Sieve in the remaining flour then and fold into the mixture with the cherries and almonds.

Turn into a 600 g greased and floured loaf tin, levelling the top with a spatula.

Bake in the pre heated oven for 45 mins or until the cake has turned golden brown and has cooked.

Leave in the tin for 5 minutes, then turn out onto a cooling tray.

When the cake has cooled, make the glace by beating the honey into the icing sugar.

Add sufficient cold water to give a flowing consistency.

Spoon the icing over the cake and allow it to drip naturally down the sides.

Arrange the cherries and almonds attractively on the top and drizzle a little of the icing over them.

Cardammon *Cake*

The addition of the cardammon in this cake imparts an unusual flavour. By adding a lemon flavoured icing it will give a refreshing edge.

Ingredients
115 g   4 oz butter
225 g – 8 oz caster sugar
2 tsp ground cardammon
1 beaten egg
125 ml – 4 fl oz single cream
300 g – 10 oz self raising flour

Icing
1 tbsp lemon juice
115 g – 4 oz icing sugar

Method
350˚F – 180˚C - Gas Mark 4

Melt the butter and pour over the sugar in a bowl Using an electric mixer, beat in the cardammon, egg and cream. Gradually stir in the sifted flour with a metal spoon.

Grease a 23 cm - 9" tin and dust sparingly with flour.

Bake in a moderate oven for 45 mins until golden brown.

Leave in the tin for a couple of minutes then turn out onto a cooling tray.

When the cake has cooled completely, blend the lemon juice into the icing sugar to make a thick icing. Spoon this over the cake allowing it to drip over the sides.

Decorate with frosted lemon slices.

*A chocolate **Layered** Cake filled with apricot puree*

Olive *Oil Fruit Cake*

Increasing popular oil used for cooking, but have you tried using it in baking?

Ingredients

225 g – 8 oz self raising flour
55 g – 2 oz caster sugar
125 ml – 4 fl oz milk
4 tbsp orange juice
150 ml – 5 fl oz olive oil
115 g – 4 oz mixed dried fruit
25 g – 1 oz pine nuts

Method

350˚F – 180˚C - Gas Mark 4

In a mixing bowl, sift the flour and stir in the caster sugar.

Pour in the milk and orange juice.

Stir the mixture using a wooden spoon and beat in the flour and sugar.

Pour in the olive oil stirring all the time and mix all the ingredients well together.

Stir in the mixed dry fruit and pine nuts then mix gently together.

Prepare a 18cm - 7" round cake tin by greasing lightly.

Spoon in the mixture and bake in a pre heated oven.

After about 45 minutes the cake should be golden and firm to the touch.

Leave the cake for a few minutes then transfer to a cooling tray to cool.

The olive is a small, hard stoned fruit of the sub tropical tree, which probably originated around the Middle East as well as the Mediterranean. Over the years it became widely available in the tropical and sub tropical areas throughout the world. One of the earliest fruits recognised by man and one which is also mentioned in the Holy Quran, known in Arabic as "Zaytoon."

There are two main types of olives. The green ones which are pickled whilst still immature and the black ones which are allowed to ripen and darken on the tree before it is plucked. Both are pickled in brine before being sold. Sometimes the green olives are stuffed, usually with chopped pimento or anchovies. However, the most important product is the oil which is extracted by crushing the fruit. It is then processed to make probably what is the most popular single oil in the world. The oils are extracted only from the ripe olives.

The oil from the first pressing is referred to as virgin oil, other varieties are a mixture of refined and virgin oils. Widely used in salad as well as fish dishes but healthy and light enough to use in baking too.

Layered *Cake*

Can be made within an hour, two easy but delicious cakes layered with icing.

Ingredients

175 g – 6 oz butter
175 g – 6 oz caster sugar
3 large eggs
150 g – 5 oz self raising flour
25 g – 1 oz cocoa powder
1/4 tsp baking powder
Pinch of salt
1 Chocolate flake

Method

375˚F – 190˚C - Gas Mark 5

Cream together the butter and sugar until light and creamy.

Add the eggs one at a time and beat well together until pale in colour.

Sift in the flour, baking powder, cocoa and salt then fold gently together using a metal spoon.

Prepare 2 x 7" baking tins by lightly greasing and divide the mixture between the tins. Bake for almost 25 minutes.

When cooled completely sandwich together with the icing of your choice. (Icings page 10)

Cakes & Buns

Peanut *Butter Cake*

Crunchy and delicious at the same time.

Ingredients

55 g – 2 oz marg
115 g – 4 oz peanut butter
225 g – 8 oz caster sugar
1/2 tsp vanilla
2 well beaten eggs
225 g – 8 oz plain flour
1/4 tsp baking soda
Pinch of salt
150 ml – 5 fl oz water
55 g – 2 oz plain chocolate

Icing

55 g – 2 oz plain chocolate
85 g – 3 oz peanut butter
150 ml – 5 fl oz single cream
25 g – 1 oz caster sugar

Method

350˚F – 180˚C - Gas Mark 4

Cream together the margarine and sugar then add the peanut butter.

Beat well until very light and fluffy.

Add the vanilla and eggs and continue beating.

In a small pan melt the chocolate on a low heat then add this to the mixture and mix well together.

In a separate bowl sift the flour and the soda, and add the salt.

Fold this alternatively into the mixture with the hot water.

Prepare two 20 cm - 8" lightly greased tins and bake for 35 minutes in a preheated oven.

The cakes should then be ready. Allow to cool for a few minutes in the baking tray then transfer onto a wire rack.

Make the icing by melting the chocolate and the peanut butter together. Add the cream and sugar and stir for a few minutes constantly until it begins to look like fudge. Cool slightly and beat until creamy. Sandwich the cake together with a thick layer of the icing then allow to set.

Mint *Choc Cake*

Mint and chocolate always team up well giving a refreshing taste.

Ingredients

175 g – 6 oz margarine
175 g – 6 oz caster sugar
1/2 tsp vanilla essence
3 well beaten eggs
115 g – 4 oz self raising flour
55 g – 2 oz cocoa powder
1 tbsp warm water

Icing

85 g – 3 oz butter
175 g – 6 oz icing sugar
1/2 tsp peppermint essence
Green food colouring

Method

375˚F – 190˚C - Gas Mark 5

Cream together the margarine and sugar in a bowl. When the mixture is light and fluffy, beat in the vanilla, and add the eggs gradually until the mixture has become thick and creamy. Sift in the flour and cocoa with a metal spoon then gently stir in the water mixing well.

Grease two 7" sandwich tins together and lightly dust with flour shaking out the access. Divide the mixture equally into these tins and bake in a pre heated oven for 25 minutes, or until thoroughly cooked and springy to the touch.

Remove the cakes from the oven and turn upside down cooling on a wire tray.

Meanwhile make the icing by beating together all the ingredients. Cream together the two cakes with the icing in between. Finally dust some icing sugar over the top.

Semolina *Cake*

Make this delicious cake extra special by tinting pink, covering with mock icing and drizzling strawberry sauce over it.

Ingredients

225 g – 8 oz caster sugar
6 eggs
250 g – 9 oz fine semolina
Finely grated rind of a lemon
85 g – 3 oz ground rice
2 tsp baking powder
Pinch of salt
4 tbsp lemon juice
55 g – 2 oz blanched almonds

Syrup

10 green cardammon pods
1 stick of cinnamon
1 strip of lemon rind
450 g – 1 lb caster sugar
300 ml – 10 fl oz water

Method

350°F – 180°C - Gas Mark 4

To make the cake put all the ingredients, except the almonds in a mixing bowl.

Beat thoroughly until the mixture is thick and pale.

Pour into a greased 23 cm - 9" square cake tin.

Bake for 1.5 hours until firm and golden brown.

Remove the cake from the oven and cool completely.

Half way through the cooking time, arrange the almonds over the top and continue cooking.

Meanwhile make the syrup by putting all the ingredients in a saucepan with the water and heat gently until the sugar has dissolved completely.

Bring to the boil and simmer for 10 minutes.

Strain and cool. When the cake has finished baking then pour the syrup over the cake and leave in the tin to absorb all the liquid.

A farmer was driving along in the countryside with his truck full of fertiliser.

The little girl who was playing with her dolls in front of her house shouted, "Hey mister, what do you have in your truck?"
"Fertiliser," the farmer replied smiling back.
"What are you going to do with it?" she asked.
"Put it on strawberries," answered the farmer.
"You should come for tea at my house, my mum puts sugar and cream on ours." She advised helpfully.

Cappuccino*Cake*

This cake is a must for the chocoholics in society. Irresistible dark chocolate and coffee cake with a frothy cream and cocoa topping.

Ingredients

225 g – 8 oz plain chocolate
1 tbsp instant coffee granules
225 g – 8 oz butter
225 g – 8 oz soft brown sugar
5 eggs – well beaten
115 g – 4 oz ground almonds
115 g – 4 oz corn flour
3 tbsp strong, black, cooled coffee
1 tbsp boiled milk

Topping

300 ml – 1/2 pt whipping cream
1 tbsp strong black coffee
Cocoa powder

Method

350°F – 180°C - Gas mark 4

Break the chocolate into small pieces and melt in a bowl over a pan of simmering water, with the instant coffee then stir well.

Beat the butter and sugar together until pale and fluffy. Beat in the eggs a little at a time then fold in the almonds, corn flour and chocolate mixture.

Pour this mixture into a greased and lined 23 cm - 9" round spring form tin.

Bake in the pre heated oven for 1 hour and 15 minutes or until risen and firm to the touch. Cover the cake with grease proof paper if necessary to prevent it becoming too brown. Allow the cake to cool in the tin.

When cold, prick the cake all over with a skewer. Mix the coffee and milk together then pour evenly over the cake. Leave to soak for about 40 minutes.

Remove the cake from the tin and transfer to a serving plate.

Make the topping by whipping the cream with the strong coffee until it just holds its shape. Spread the cream evenly on top and sift some cocoa powder over the top for decoration.

A woman in the diet club was lamenting that she gained weight rather then losing some.

She said that she'd made her family's favourite cake over the weekend and that the family had eaten over half of it.

The next day she'd kept staring at the other half, until finally she cut a thin slice for herself. One slice led to another, and soon the whole cake was gone. The woman went on to tell how upset she was with her lack of willpower, and that she knew her family would be disappointed. So to avoid that disappointment, she'd spent the next morning baking and icing another cappuccino cake. She then ate half of it and left the other half untouched, just like the night before in the fridge!

Nobody found out and nobody would!

Sponge *Cake*

This is a simple cake, which is so easy and quick to prepare. The secret is making it special by filling it with exotic fruit.

Ingredients

85 g – 3 oz self raising flour
3 eggs
85 g – 3 oz caster sugar
1 tbsp hot water

Filling

3 tbsp apricot or red jam
Sifted icing sugar
Fresh or canned fruit to fill
(strawberries, kiwi, mandarin)

Method

350˚F – 180˚C - Gas Mark 4

Sieve the flour several times onto grease proof paper. With an electric mixer, mix the eggs and sugar on a high speed until thick and creamy. Sprinkle the flour over the top and fold in very gently with a metal spoon. Finally stir in the hot water.

Grease two 7" sandwich tins, then divide the mixture into the tins. Bake in a pre heated oven for about 20 minutes, then leave to cool for a few minutes.

Turn out onto a cooling tray and when cold, sandwich together with the jam, fruit and sifted icing sugar. You may decorate the top of the cake in the same way.

Apricots are known as a natural and colourful fruit. It is a most popular and well recognised fruit used in the bakers kitchen. Perhaps more importantly it is used as a jam, jelly or a conserve. Apricot jam plays an important role in the finishing of many cakes as well as being used as a spread to join cake layers together.

The boiled apricot glace can give cakes a smooth, hard surface on which softer compounds such as chocolate and fondants can be spread without being soaked and sucked into the cake. Danish pastries are often glaced to give a shiny appearance and a slight tangy taste.

Apricots originated in China and have been cultivated in the temperate zone for some 2000 years. They are available in a variety of forms, fresh, dried, preserved in jams and as a cordial drink. The attractive fruit has only one stone to which the flesh does not cling and within this stone is a kernel which is used in the production of almond paste. The kernel looks similar to that of an almond kernel and contains a rich oil which is often used as a substitute for almond oil and more often associated with facial washes and cosmetic uses. When purchasing apricots, be sure to choose the ones with a warm, orange-red tone to the skin.

Fudge *Cake*

This rich cake, covered in fudge icing can be served as a special treat or even as a dessert at the end of a meal. It may seem like a long process but wait till the end result is achieved!

Ingredients

115 g – 4 oz dark cooking chocolate
225 ml – 8 fl oz milk
175 g – 6 oz light brown sugar
3 egg yolks
300 g – 10 oz sifted plain flour
1 tsp bicarbonate of soda
Pinch of salt
115 g – 4 oz butter
175 g – 6 oz caster sugar
60 ml – 2 fl oz water
1 tsp vanilla essence
2 egg whites

Method

350°F – 180°C - Gas Mark 4

Put the chocolate, milk, brown sugar and one egg yolk into a Pyrex bowl placed over a saucepan of boiling water. Cook the mixture in this way stirring continually until you will find that the mixture has thickened slightly and the chocolate has melted.

Then remove from the heat and set aside. Sift the flour and the bicarbonate of soda several times into a medium sized bowl with the salt.

In another bowl, cream the butter and gradually add the caster sugar, beating well until light and fluffy.

Add the remaining egg yolks one at a time and beat in well after each addition.

Gently mix in a 1/3 of the flour, followed by 1/2 of the water. Add the remaining flour and water like this and mix well until the batter is very smooth and silky.

Stir in the vanilla essence, then add the chocolate mixture. Beat the egg whites until they form stiff peaks, then with a metal spoon fold in lightly.

Grease three 20 cm - 8 inch loose bottomed cake tins with some melted butter and line with grease proof paper cut into circles of the same size. Grease again. Divide the mixture equally into three and bake for 25 minutes.

Remove the tins from the oven and cool on a cooling tray.

Decorate with a double quantity of fudge frosting. (see icings - page 10)

Sandwich the cakes together with the fudge icing using a palette knife making a swirling pattern and add shelled walnuts to decorate.

Carrot *Buns*

The clever combination of carrots and the tangy scent of the tangerine make these buns a delight to bake and eat.

Ingredients

175 g – 6 oz freshly grated carrots
175 g – 6 oz soft brown sugar
200 ml – 7 fl oz sunflower oil
2 well beaten eggs
175 g – 6 oz plain wholewheat flour
55 g – 2 oz ground almonds
55 g – 2 oz wheat germ
2 tsp caraway seeds
1 tsp bicarbonate of soda
Rind of two tangerines

Method

325°F – 170°C - Gas Mark 3

Place the grated carrots in a large bowl. Then in the order that you read the ingredients, add them one by one and mix together gently.

Divide the mixture equally between 16 paper cases and bake in the centre of a pre heated oven.

After about half an hour, check to see that the are well risen and firm to the touch.

Remove and cool on a wire tray.

Walnut *Cake*

A deliciously flavoured cake using corn oil and walnuts.

Ingredients

3 eggs
85 g – 3 oz caster sugar
85 g – 3 oz self raising flour
2 tbsp corn oil
115 g – 4 oz finely chopped walnuts

Filling

115 g – 4 oz butter
150 g – 5 oz sifted icing sugar
1/2 tsp vanilla essence
A little milk

Frosting

400 g – 1lb granulated sugar
150 ml – 5 fl oz water
2 egg whites
10 walnut halves

Method

350°F – 180°C - Gas Mark 4

Whisk the eggs and sugar until they are thick and leave a trail when lifted up.

Sieve in the flour and fold in with a metal spoon.

Add the corn oil and the finely chopped walnuts.

Divide the mixture between two 7 inch sandwich tins which have been greased and lined with paper. Level the mixture with a spatula and bake in a pre heated oven for about 25 minutes until the cakes are baked.

Leave to cool for a couple of minutes in the tin, then turn out and cool on a wire tray.

When the cakes are cold, split each one into half. Make the filling by creaming together the butter and the icing sugar, then beat in the vanilla and enough milk to make a spreadable mixture. Spread the filling on just three surfaces and pile on top of each other. For the icing, put the sugar and water into a heavy saucepan and heat gently until the sugar has dissolved. Boil rapidly until you reach 250°F or until the mixture forms a hard ball when dropped into a glass of cold water.

Remove from the heat. Whisk the egg whites until very stiff, then continue beating with an electric whisk and pour in the syrup gradually.

Continue until it is thick enough to spread, then quickly spread it all over the top and sides of the cake and decorate with walnut halves.

The icing will then harden and set giving it a frosty sheen.

Walnuts are native to the Asian region and are one of the most commonly consumed nuts in the world. They were used for trading during the Persian empire, and many cultures believed that the consumption of walnuts were beneficial to the health and in warding of evil spirits and bad luck.

Walnuts grow on a walnut tree inside green pods which turn brown and almost woodlike when they dry.

They are delicious eaten whole but are also used as a powder, or ground and chopped.

Cakes & Buns

Ingredients *used in my recipies*

Saffron *Buns*

Delicious small buns, including one of the world's most exotic spices.

Ingredients

225 g – 8 oz flour
1 tsp baking powder
Pinch of salt
1/4 tsp ground saffron
225 g – 8 oz butter
225 g – 8 oz soft brown sugar
3 eggs
175 g – 6 oz dried apricots, finely chopped
1 tsp rose water

Method

375 °F – 190 °C - Gas Mark 5

Sift the flour, baking powder, salt and saffron into a mixing bowl.

Cream the butter and sugar until soft and creamy. Add the beaten eggs slowly making sure they don't curdle, then add the rose water. Using a metal spoon fold in the remaining mixture and the apricots ensuring that all the ingredients are well mixed.

Arrange 20 bun cases on a tray and fill each case with 2 tbsp of the mixture.

Bake in a pre heated oven for 20 minutes, until golden brown.

Saffron is made from the dried stigma of a species from the crocus family. The bulb grows about 15 cm - 6 inches high and has purple flowers in autumn.

It is estimated that over 4,000 blooms are required to yield 25 g - 1 oz of saffron.

Now you can see why saffron is recognised as the most expensive spice in the world. It has been used for centuries for flavourings and colour, but is also effective as a stimulant and digestive, it increases the flow of saliva as well as promoting perspiration. It is considered a 'hot' spice. The Romans used it to bathe in and as a vital ingredients in their oils to perfume their bodies.

Romans introduced saffron to England, and it was cultivated for a few hundred years in Essex, well known as Saffron Walden. But the Spanish saffron is considered the best and it was the Arabs that introduced the spice to the Spaniards.

Nowadays it is cultivated in many countries but nothing can really match the pure saffron from Spain.

In many countries turmeric, marigold stamens or other similar ones are added to increase the weight. These are not pure and should not be bought.

Saffron is expensive, therefore, it is used in minute quantities. There is no such thing as cheap saffron!

Maximise the flavour and colouring by gently toasting the strands in a metal spoon over a cooker, then crushing or pounding them. Infuse in hot water or milk and leave for a few minutes.

It is advisable to buy the whole threads rather then the powdered form.

Cakes & Buns

Sesame *Cake*

This cake is unusual in the sense that it contains sesame seeds for the topping rather then nuts and coconut.

Ingredients

300 g – 10 oz plain flour
2 tsp baking powder
55 g – 2 oz ground almonds
225 g – 8 oz softened butter
200 g – 7 oz sugar
3 eggs
150 ml – 5 fl oz fresh orange juice
55 g – 2 oz whole blanched almonds
1 tbsp sesame seeds

Method

350°F – 180°C - Gas Mark 4

Sift the flour and baking powder into a basin and stir in the ground almonds.

In another bowl cream together the butter and sugar until light and fluffy.

Then beat in the eggs one at a time using an electric mixer.

Fold in the flour mixture alternating with the orange juice until evenly mixed together. Prepare a 23 cm - 9" square cake tin and line with greased paper.

Spoon the mixture into this tin and even out the surface.

Arrange the whole blanched almonds over the top and sprinkle the sesame seeds.

Bake in the centre of the oven for almost 55 minutes.

Take out of the oven and leave to cool for 5 minutes, then remove from the tin and peel of the paper. Cut into diamond shapes.

Toffee *Topped Cakes*

These cakes are really popular with children and adults alike.

Ingredients

225 g – 8 oz plain wholewheat flour
1 tsp baking powder
115 g – 4 oz soft light brown sugar
115 g – 4 oz margarine
115 g – 4 oz chopped dates
85 g – 3 oz chopped walnuts
2 well beaten eggs
1-2 tbsp milk - if required

Topping

85 g – 3 oz soft brown sugar
40 g – 1.5 oz margarine
2 tbsp single cream
55 g – 2 oz chopped walnuts

Method

350°F – 180°C - Gas Mark 4

Combine the flour, baking powder and sugar in a large bowl. Rub the margarine until it resembles fine breadcrumbs. Stir in the dates and walnuts, then the beaten eggs until it is a soft dropping consistency. You may need to add the milk if it isn't soft enough.

Place 16 bun cases in a bun tin and divide the mixture evenly between these cases.

Bake in the centre of a hot oven for almost 30 minutes or until well risen and firm to the touch.

Remove from the oven then cool on a tray.

Prepare the topping only when the cakes have cooled, because the topping will set quickly then the nuts won't stick to the top.

Combine the sugar, margarine and cream together in a small saucepan.

Bring to the boil stirring gently all the time for about 3 minutes or until it has darkened slightly. Spoon a little topping over the buns and let it drizzle over the sides then quickly turn and dip into the chopped walnuts. Leave to set completely.

**TIP: You can use a variety of nuts and coconut etc for the decoration.

Snow *Cake*

A delicious and light cake, giving a soft appearance with the white coconut.

Ingredients

125 g – 5 oz margarine
125 g – 5 oz caster sugar
3 eggs
225 g – 8 oz self raising flour
Pinch of salt
115 g – 4 oz desiccated coconut
3 tbsp milk

Topping
Buttercream
Desiccated coconut

Method

350˚F – 180˚C - Gas Mark 4

Cream together the margarine and butter until very light. Beat in the eggs one at a time, beating well after each addition. Sift the flour and salt and then mix with the coconut.

Add these dry ingredients to the creamy mixture alternately with the milk.

Lightly grease an 18 cm- 7" cake tin. Turn the mixture into this tin and bake in a pre heated oven for just over an hour.

When it has baked, cool in the tray for about 10 minutes then cool on a wire tray.

Spread the cake with butter cream and cover completely with dessicated coconut.

Lemington *Squares*

This delicious recipe won me a prize in the Blackburn Citizen when I entered my first competition. Sharp slices of cakes, dipped in a delicious coating of cocoa and coconut.

Ingredients

225 g – 8 oz butter
350 g – 12 oz caster sugar
4 eggs
350 g – 12 oz plain flour
1 tsp baking powder
1 tsp cream of tarter
1 cup of milk
Desiccated coconut

Coating
2 cups of boiling water
350 g – 12 oz caster sugar
4 tbsp cocoa powder
115 g – 4 oz butter
Few drops of vanilla essence

Method

375˚F – 190˚C - Gas Mark 5

Make the cake by creaming the butter and sugar together until light and fluffy.

Beat in the eggs one at a time adding a spoon of sifted flour with each egg.

Fold in the flour and baking powder. Finally add the milk and stir into the mixture lightly. Pour into a lightly greased square baking tin, and bake in a pre heated oven for about 40 minutes.

The cake should be lightly golden and when a skewer is inserted should come out clean. Leave in the tin and allow to cool completely before cutting into slices.

To make the coating, boil the sugar, water and cocoa in a saucepan and bring to the boil. Once it is boiling, add the butter and vanilla. When all ingredients are melted together remove from heat and allow to cool until it is just warm.

The coating will be thin and runny. Cut the cake into individual size squares. Dip the slices individually in the coating and then immediately roll in the coconut flakes. Stand on a cake rack until they have cooled completely and set.

Serve on it's own or with ice cream.

**TIP: It will be easier to coat the cake if the baked cake is frozen. Then after coating allow to thaw at room temperature.

Vegan *Nut Cake*

This cake is ideal for vegans because it contains no eggs or other dairy products.

Ingredients

350 g – 12 oz plain wholewheat flour
1 tsp mixed spice
175 g – 6 oz soya margarine
200 g – 7 oz muscavado sugar
175 g – 6 oz sultanas
175 g – 6 oz raisins
175 g – 6 oz currants
85 g – 3 oz mixed peel
150 g – 5 oz glace cherries, halved
Grated zest of a lemon
2 tbsp ground almonds
25 g – 1 oz chopped almonds
125 ml – 4 fl oz soya milk
75 ml – 3 fl oz sunflower
2 tbsp malt vinegar
1 tbsp bicarbonate of soda

Topping
225 g – 8 oz mixed (pistachio, pecan and walnuts)
4 tbsp clear light honey

Method
400˚F – 200˚C - Gas Mark 6

Sift the flour and mixed spices into a bowl, add in the bran left in the sieve.

Rub the margarine into the flour until it resembles fine breadcrumbs.

Stir in the sugar, dried fruits, mixed peels, cherries, orange zest and the ground and blanched almonds.

Warm 50 ml - 2 fl oz of the soya milk in a sauce pan and add the sunflower oil and vinegar.

Dissolve the bicarbonate of soda in the rest of the milk and combine the two mixtures, stir into the dry ingredients.

Prepare a spring form square tin with a double thickness of greased paper.

Spoon the cake mixture into the tin and level out with a table knife. Bake in the centre of the oven for almost 2.5 hours, test with a skewer before taking out of the oven.

Leave in the tin for 5 minutes and then turn onto a wire tray, peeling off the paper and allowing the cake to cool completely. Pile all the fruit on top of the cake and glaze with the warmed honey.

Double *Chocolate Muffins*

A classic recipe for an increasingly popular cake. Quick to make and delicious served fresh from the oven.

Ingredients

115 g – 4 oz plain chocolate
55 g – 2 oz cocoa powder
225 g – 8 oz self raising flour
1 tsp baking powder
55 g – 2 oz dark brown soft sugar
Pinch of salt
115 g – 4 oz plain chocolate dots
255 ml – 8 fl oz milk
4 tbsp vegetable oil
1 tsp vanilla essence
1 egg

Method
425˚F – 320˚C - Gas Mark 7

Break the chocolate into small pieces and melt gently over a saucepan.

Remove from the heat and stir in the remaining ingredients. With an electric whisk beat thoroughly together then spoon the mixture into the paper cases.

Spoon into large muffin cases and place the cases into a thoroughly greased large 12 hole muffin or bun tin.

Bake in a pre heated oven for 15 minutes. They should be well risen and firm to the touch. Serve warm.

Semolina *Cake with mock icing and strawberry sauce*

Biscuits & Slices

Almond Slices
Apple Shortbread
Apricot Slices
Caraway Biscuits
Choc Chip Biscuits
Chocolate Biscuits
Chocolate PinWheels
Coconut Ice
Coconut Slices
Cornflake Biscuits
Custard Biscuits
Date Slices

Delicious Biscuits
Easy Chocolate Slices
European Biscuits
Fig & Nut Biscuits
Ginger Slices
Hazelnut Biscuits
Honey Biscuits
Honey Nut Diamonds
Honey Pineapple Slices
Karachi Biscuits
Lemon Creams
Light Biscuits

Maryland Biscuits
Nest Biscuits
Novelty Wheels
Nutty Slices
Nutty Wonders
Oat Crunchies
Orange Biscuits
Orange Peanut Biscuits
Papaya Biscuits
Passion Fruit Biscuits
Poppy Seed Wheels
Quick Biscuits

Red Cherry Biscuits
Ring Biscuits
Romany Creams
Sesame Seed Slices
Star Biscuits
Traditional Coconut
Biscuits
Treacle Nut Biscuits
Trifle Fingers
Viennese Whirls
Walnut Diamonds
Walnut Wonders

Delicious *Biscuits p47*

Chocolate *Biscuits*

These biscuits are delicious on their own but even better if creamed together.

Ingredients

225 g – 8 oz butter
115 g – 4 oz caster sugar
225 g – 8 oz self raising flour
1 tsp cinnamon powder
55 g – 2 oz cocoa
1 tsp vanilla essence

....

Method

350°F – 180°C - Gas Mark 4

....

Cream the butter until it is light and fluffy. Add the sugar gradually until the colour is very pale. Sift in the flour, cinnamon powder and cocoa, stir in a little at a time until it is smooth. Finally add the vanilla essence.

With your hands roll about a teaspoon of the dough into a small ball and place on the lightly greased baking sheet.

Dip a fork into cold water and flatten the balls slightly with the back of the fork.

Continue doing this with the mixture placing the balls two inches apart.

Bake in an oven for 10-12 minutes.

Allow to cool slightly on the tray before lifting off onto a cooling tray.

Cream together with either butter icing or any light cream.

Vanilla was introduced in Europe when discovered in Mexico where the Aztecs had been using vanilla pods in the production of chocolate.

Vanilla Essence is made by soaking the pods in pure alcohol to extract the flavouring. Brown colouring is added to give the essence an attractive appearance.

Vanillin is a synthetic flavour which is subtler then the natural product.

The alcohol is cleverly disguised and in chemical terms is better known as 'propylene glycol' or as 'as ethanol alcohol.' I don't want to start a national panic for those of us who don't consume alcohol in any form, but vanilla essence and flavouring does contain minute amounts of alcohol. I cross checked with various companies, pharmacists and manufacturers who confirmed this. I was surprised myself having used this product for years but if you are worried you may want to check yourself. But vanilla pods are not expensive and last a good few months. The fruit of a Mexican climbing orchid and growing 12-20 cm in length. It is picked while still in its green stage and cured and dried until black and aromatic. Once dried the pods must be kept in air tight jars to retain their flavours.

The pods are often used in sauces and cremes by boiling with milk and cream and then being allowed to infuse for some time. You can remove and wash for reusing.

Use to replace vanilla essence and flavouring in all recipes if desired.

Biscuits & Slices

Apricot *Slices*

These apricot slices taste delicious and carry a unique taste. The natural colour of the apricots add that extra visual appeal.

Ingredients

115 g – 4 oz margarine
115 g – 4 oz dried apricots, soaked overnight
55 g – 2 oz caster sugar
175 g – 6 oz flour
1/2 tsp baking powder
1/4 tsp salt
2 eggs
225 g – 8 oz brown sugar
1/2 tsp vanilla essence
85 g – 3 oz walnuts finely chopped
55 g – 2 oz icing sugar

Method

350 ˚F – 180 ˚C - Gas Mark 4

Drain the apricots and chop them into small pieces.

In a large mixing bowl, cream the margarine and sugar together until light and creamy.

Rub 115 g - 4 oz of flour into the mixture until it resembles fine breadcrumbs. Press this mixture into a lightly greased baking sheet, and bake in a pre heated oven for about 25 minutes until golden.

Meanwhile combine the remaining flour, with the baking flour and salt.

In a second bowl gradually beat the eggs into the brown sugar and whisk thoroughly.

Add this to the flour mixture and stir constantly adding the vanilla essence chopped apricots and walnuts. Spread this over the top of the cooked pastry layer in the tin. Bake for a further 30 minutes. Remove the tin from the oven and cool.

Slice into preferred sizes and roll in icing sugar. Delicious served warm or cold.

Caraway *Biscuits*

These light biscuits are ideal to eat on their own or with cheese and they don't contain any sugar.

Ingredients

55 g – 2 oz butter
115 g – 4 oz plain flour
Pinch of salt
1 egg
1 tbsp water
4 tsp caraway seeds
1/2 egg yolk, lightly beaten

Method

375 ˚F – 190 ˚C - Gas Mark 5

In a mixing bowl beat the 55 g – 2 oz butter and the oil with half of the sugar.

Into this mixture, beat the eggs until light and creamy, then whisk in the milk.

Sift the flour, baking powder, salt, cinnamon powder and fold all together with a metal spoon.

Spoon this mixture into twelve cake cases and bake for 25 minutes. After this time the cakes should be lightly golden.

Take out from the oven and immediately brush the melted butter over them.

Sprinkle the powdered cinnamon, and caster sugar for that extra flavour.

Almond *Slices*

The almond topping make these slices really delicious.

Ingredients
175 g – 6 oz plain flour
115 g – 4 oz butter
55 g – 2 oz caster sugar
1 egg yolk

Topping
2 tbsp apricot jam
1 egg white
85 g – 3 oz icing sugar
Flaked almonds

Method
350°F – 180°C - Gas Mark 4

In a mixing bowl, rub the butter into the flour and sugar. Bind the mixture together with the beaten egg yolk and then roll into a rectangle about a 1/4" thick.

Brush with warmed jam.

Then make a meringue with the egg white and icing sugar by whisking together until soft peaks form.

Spread this over the jam and sprinkle with the flaked nuts.

Bake in a lightly greased baking sheet for 40 mins in a pre heated oven.

Cut with a sharp knife into slices and cool on a wire tray.

Store in an air tight tin.

Apple *Shortbread*

Melting shortcake biscuits with a centre of moist and spicy stewed apple. Almost a cross between a pie and a biscuit.

Ingredients
300 g – 10 oz unsalted butter
300 g – 10 oz caster sugar
3 eggs
300 g – 10 oz plain flour
1 tsp baking powder
1 tsp ground cinnamon
1 tsp mixed spice
300 g – 10 oz lightly stewed apple, well drained
85 g – 3 oz icing sugar

Method
350°F – 180°C - Gas Mark 4

Cream the butter and sugar until very light. Then add the eggs one at a time beating well after each addition. Continue mixing until well combined and then sift the flour, baking powder and the spice into the mixture. Continue mixing until all is well incorporated.

Spread half of this mixture evenly in a lightly greased and lined 18 x 28 cm baking tray. Spread the stewed apple evenly over the top then carefully cover the top with the remaining cake mixture.

Bake in a pre heated oven for 50 minutes. Cool in the tray and dust with icing sugar. Slice as required.

Delicious *Biscuits*

Here's a delicious buttery and crunchy biscuit decorated with coloured jam.

Ingredients
115 g – 4 oz butter
150 g – 5 oz plain flour
55 g – 2 oz caster sugar
55 g – 2 oz semolina

Glace
Few drops green colouring
4 tbsp red jam

Method
350˚F – 180˚C - Gas Mark 4

Rub the butter into the sifted flour using your fingertips. Add the sugar, semolina and the salt. Form into a pliable dough adding a little milk if the mixture is too dry.

Roll into 1/4" thickness and cut into circles using a cutter.

Arrange on a lightly greased baking tray and bake for almost 15 minutes taking care not to brown. They should be cooked but still light in colour.

Cool completely on a wire tray.

Heat the jam until quite liquidy then divide into two.

To one half add the food colouring and mix well.

Taking a fine cocktail stick, dip into the jam and decorate as you like.

**TIP: Instead of the jam try using white and dark chocolate for decoration.

Maryland *Biscuits*

Simple to make with the irresistible taste of the nuts and chocolate chips.

Ingredients
175 g – 6 oz marg
175 g – 6 oz sugar
175 g – 6 oz brown sugar
Vanilla essence
2 eggs
12 oz self raising flour
115 g – 4 oz chopped nuts
175 g – 6 oz chocolate chips

Method
350˚F – 180˚C - Gas Mark 4

In a mixing bowl cream the marg, sugar and vanilla.

Beat in the eggs then fold in the rest of the ingredients.

Lightly grease a baking sheet and drop tablespoons of this mixture onto the sheet.

Leave enough space between them to allow for spreading.

Bake in a pre heated oven for almost 15 mins or until cooked and lightly golden.

Cool for a few minutes on the tray before transferring onto a cooling tray. Store in an air tight container.

**TIP: Melt milk and white chocolate and drizzle over the biscuits, allow to set.

Quick *Biscuits*

Just four simple ingredients can create delicious results.

Ingredients
450 g – 1 lb butter
150 g – 5 oz icing sugar
150 g – 5 oz custard power
Enough self raising flour to make a
Soft biscuit dough

Method
375°F – 190°C - Gas Mark 5

In a large mixing bowl, cream the butter and sugar well.

Sift in the custard powder and gradually add enough sifted self raising flour to make a soft biscuit dough. Using a biscuit maker, press out into required shapes onto a lightly greased baking sheet. Alternatively roll out onto a lightly floured board and cut into attractive shapes. Decorate with hundreds and thousands, chopped cherries or angelica and bake for almost 25 minutes until lightly golden.

Cool on a wire tray. Whilst still warm brush with glace icing for that little shine.

Romany *Creams*

The old time favourite at eid and other occasions.

Ingredients
225 g – 8 oz butter
300 g – 10 oz sugar
1 tsp cocoa
3 eggs
3 tsp baking powder
150 g – 5 oz desiccated coconut
1 tsp vanilla essence
450 g – 1 lb self raising flour

Method
350°F – 180°C - Gas Mark 4

In a large bowl, mix together the flour, baking powder, sugar and cocoa. Add the butter and vanilla then using the rub in method, make the mixture resemble fine breadcrumbs. Add the coconut and mix. Whisk the egg and use this to bind the whole mixture together into a biscuit dough. If the mixture is a little dry add a tbsp of milk.

Roll out onto a lightly floured board and cut into shapes, or use a biscuit press.

Place on a lightly greased baking tray and bake in the pre heated oven for about 15 minutes.

Cream together with chocolate flavoured butter icing.

Orange *Peanut Biscuits*

A sparkling experience with the refreshing taste of orange.

Ingredients
150 g – 5 oz self raising flour
Pinch of cinnamon powder
115 g – 4 oz marg
115 g – 4 oz caster sugar
2 tsp undiluted orange squash
115 g – 4 oz salted peanuts

Method
350°F – 180°C - Gas Mark 4

Sift the flour and the cinnamon together and mix in the nuts. Cream the margarine with the sugar and then beat in the orange squash. Fold in the flour, cinnamon and peanuts a metal spoon to make a soft dough.

Take small pieces of dough and roll into balls. Flatten slightly with a fork to make an imprint and place on a lightly greased baking sheet.

Bake for just 12 minutes, by which time a wonderful aroma should fill your kitchen. Transfer onto a cooling tray. Store in an airtight container when cooled completely.

Custard *Biscuits*

Traditional biscuits can be transformed by using assorted decorations.

Ingredients
225 g – 8 oz butter
8 tbsp sugar
1 tsp vanilla essence
2 eggs
600 g – 1lb 5 oz plain flour
4 tsp baking powder
8 tbsp custard powder

Method
375 °F – 190 °C - Gas Mark 5

Beat the butter and sugar together until creamy. Add the eggs beating well after each addition and then the vanilla.

Sift in the flour and the powders and knead well together to make a soft biscuit dough. Using a biscuit maker, press out into required shapes onto a lightly greased baking sheet. Alternatively roll out onto a lightly floured board and cut into attractive shapes. Decorate with hundreds and thousands or angelica and bake for almost 25 minutes until lightly golden.

Cool on a wire tray.

The wealthy lawyer was being driven through a country road in his sleek, polished black limousine.

Suddenly he was amazed by a strange sight and he ordered his smartly dressed chauffeur to stop. He was amazed to see some people walking around in a field just picking at grass and eating hand fulls. The chauffeur opened the door for him and he got out to investigate. "Why are you eating grass?" he asked one man. "Well sir, we are homeless, penniless and we are so hungry." the poor man replied.

The lawyer thought for a moment and looked around him. Looking back at his limo and again at the people he said to the man "Look why don't you all come with me?" "But sir, I have a wife with two children!" "Bring them along! Bring your friends too." he said pointing to another man, "You come with us too!"

"But sir, I have a wife with three children!" he answered. "Don't worry, bring them as well!" Once underway, one of the poor fellows says, "Sir, you are too kind. Thank you for taking all of us with you."

The lawyer replied, "No problem, you'll like it. You'll have more fun at my place." Everyone inside the limo was smiling at their good fortune, until he said, "the grass at my house is about a foot taller, you'll enjoy it!"

Ring *Biscuits*

Delicious biscuits which are topped with cinnamon and sugar.

Ingredients
300 g – 10 oz butter
115 g – 4 oz sugar
400 g – 14 oz self raising flour
2 egg yolks
300 g – 10 oz ground almonds

Method
375 °F – 190 °C - Gas Mark 5

Cream the butter and sugar together. Beat in the egg yolks and then sift in the flour.

Add the ground almonds and mix well together.

Prepare a lightly greased tray and pipe out using a 1/2" nozzle into neat rings.

Bake in the oven until lightly golden.

Cool on a wire tray and store in an air tight container.

**TIP: When baked, brush with glace icing and sprinkle cinnamon and sugar for extra flavour and appeal.

Passion Fruit *Biscuits*

Passion Fruit *Biscuits*

These delicious and intriguing biscuits have the seeds left in to add a crunch with a exotic influence.

Ingredients
175 g – 6 oz butter
55 g – 2 oz caster sugar
175 g – 6 oz plain flour
55 g – 2 oz corn flour
3 passion fruits

....

Method
350°F – 175°C - Gas Mark 4

....

In a large mixing bowl beat the butter and sugar until it is light and fluffy.

Sift in the two flours then with your hands mix to a firm dough.

Cut the fruit in half and scoop out the pulp with a teaspoon.

Stir in the passion fruit pulp and transfer onto greaseproof paper, forming into a roll.

Cover well and chill for an hour in the refrigerator.

Lightly grease two baking sheets with vegetable oil.

Take out the roll, which should be cold and firm now and cut into 5mm - 1/2" slices.

Place them all on the baking sheets and bake in a pre heated oven for 20 minutes until lightly brown.

Allow 5 minutes on the baking sheet before transferring onto the cooling tray. Store in an airtight container.

Poppy Seed *Wheels*

A little sweet and sticky because of the jam, but appealing and delicious.

Ingredients
115 g – 4 oz softened butter or margarine
55 g   2 oz caster sugar
175 g – 6 oz plain flour
2 tbsp milk
4 tbsp plum jam
2 tbsp poppy seeds

....

Method
350°F – 175°C - Gas Mark 4

....

In a mixing bowl beat the butter and sugar until light and fluffy.

Stir in the flour and pour into the milk gradually. Use your hands and form a dough with the mixture.

Wrap in cling film and chill in the fridge for 45 minutes.

On a lightly floured board roll out the dough into a rectangle.

In a small bowl beat the jam for a few minutes until it is spreadable and smooth.

Spread evenly onto the dough and sprinkle the poppy seeds.

Roll up tightly from the longest edge, into a swiss roll shape.

Carefully cut the dough into even slices and place on a lightly greased baking tray for 15-20 minutes. Bake until lightly golden in a preheated oven.

Allow to cool slightly then transfer onto a wire tray.

Honey

Honey is a natural and magical ingredient used in many recipes. A gift from our Creator but made with the skill of the bees.

So special is the liquid that it has been mentioned in the Holy Quran.

But what exactly is this golden liquid? Where does it come from? What does it contain? What are its uses?

Honey is created by the bees that convert the sucrose, in the nectar of the flowers, into glucose and fructose by means of an enzyme that it carries in its body.

The flavour and consistency of each individual honey, comes from the variety of plants visited.

Rosemary and heather are the most prized and the honey taken from the Greek Mountain, Hymettus is a particularly famous.

Some honeys are light, golden and runny while in contrast others are rich in colour and texture.

Honey contains a complex mixture of natural sugars around 80%, water 18% and the remaining 2% will include minerals, vitamins, pollen, protein and amino acids.

But it is the balance of the natural sugars and glucose and fructose, which determines whether it remains clear or thick enough to set.

The higher the level of fructose the longer it will stay in the liquid form.

It is estimated that a hive of bees can produce around 110 kg a year.

Honey is an unquestionable source of energy and is often used by sportsman.

Have you ever wondered about the numerous ways in which honey can be used?

For baking, cooking, or for example in barbecue cooking a mix of lemon juice and honey used for basting towards end of cooking time will give a sweet and tangy flavour as well as a light sheen.

For medicinal purposes, especially recognised for curing sore throats and coughs. Either eaten on it's own or mixed with other ingredients such a dry ginger powder or lemon juice.

Honey also aids digestion as well as a natural glow to the complexion.

Useful for beauty products often included in soaps, shampoos and facial scrubs. It's natural formic acid content and enzymes are believed to contribute enormously to its antiseptic qualities.

Recognised in Egypt for embalming and in India as a preservative.

In the Mediterranean you will find honey always taking it's place at the breakfast table alongside different cheeses and olives.

Is there a better way then to start the day with a nutritional and healthy breakfast? Honey imparts a feeling of general well being and strength and vitality.

Because it is referred to as a 'hygroscopic,' which means that it attracts moisture it is perfect for baking cakes. It helps keep them moist for longer then usual, but because of this quality biscuits are known to become softer.

Honey *Pineapple Slices*

Honey and Pineapple, two compatible ingredients, can only provide successful results.

Ingredients
1 cup honey
2 tbsp vegetable oil
1 egg
350 g – 12 oz self raising flour
1 tbsp baking powder
1/2 tsp salt
55 g – 2 oz chopped roasted nuts
1 cup raw wheat bran
1 cup canned pineapple juice

Method
350°F – 180°C - Gas Mark 4

Pre heat a 9 by 5" loaf pan.

Blend together the honey, oil and the egg gradually and mix well at full speed for a few minutes.

Sift together the flour, baking powder and salt, then coat the nuts with one half of the flour.

Gradually fold in the other half to the egg mixture, then mix in the bran and pineapple juice. Finally add the remaining flour and nut mixture and mix gently but well together. Pour into a lightly greased loaf pan and bake in a pre heated oven until golden, test to see if baked then cool slightly before turning out onto a cooling tray. Serve hot or cold with honey and butter.

Karachi *Biscuits*

One of my favourite biscuits with a rich coconut filling, always a traditional favourite at festive occasions.

Ingredients
300 g – 10 oz self raising flour or as required
115 g – 4 oz butter
115 g – 4 oz icing sugar
1 tsp cardammon powder
3 tsp baking powder
Large pinch of cardammon powder
2 small eggs
Few drops of vanilla essence

Filling
115 g – 4 oz butter
2 cups of desiccated coconut
1 tsp cardammon powder

Method
350°F – 180°C - Gas Mark 4

Make the filling first by braising the ingredients together on a low heat on the cooker.

Keep stirring until the coconut has changed to a light golden colour.

Remove from the stove and allow to cool.

Make the dough by rubbing the butter into the sifted flour to resemble breadcrumbs.

Add the icing sugar, baking powder, and cardammon powder then mix well. Beat the eggs separately with the vanilla and use this to bind the dough together. Use just enough to make a pliable biscuit dough. If it's too dry then add a little milk.

Divide the dough into two.

Roll one piece out into an oblong shape with a 1/4" thickness.

Divide the filling into half also and spread one half onto this and roll up tightly like a Swiss roll.

Cover with cling film and chill for an hour or so.

Follow the same method with the 2nd half and chill.

Remove from the fridge after a few hours, then slice into required thickness and place on a lightly greased baking sheet.

Bake in a moderate oven for almost 20 minutes or until just lightly golden.

Remove and cool on a wire tray. Store in an airtight tin.

Coconut *Ice*

Coconut *Ice*

If you love coconut and have a sweet tooth, but very little time, try this!

Ingredients
500 g – icing sugar
1 x 405 g tin of condensed milk
350 g – 12 oz desiccated coconut
Red food colouring

Method

Sift the icing sugar in a bowl and mix with the condensed milk.

Stir in the desiccated coconut with a spoon and you may find the mixture a little stiff by now.

Line the base of a baking tin with greaseproof paper and dust liberally with sifted icing sugar.

Transfer half of the mixture into the tin and press down firmly with the back of a spoon.

To the rest of the mixture add a few drops of colouring, and then knead well together.

Press this on top of the mixture already in the tin and press firmly again.

Cover with cling film and leave to chill overnight. In the morning cut into slices.

You can wrap in clear cellophane and tie the ends with red ribbon like a sweet.

Coconut *Slices*

These slices are immensely popular. Crunchy and crisp with the addition of oats for extra texture.

Ingredients
115 g – 4 oz butter
85 g   3 oz soft brown sugar
85 g – 3 oz desiccated coconut
115 g – 4 oz rolled oats
6 tbsp cornflakes
1 tbsp clear honey

Method
325˚F – 170˚C - Gas Mark 3

Mix together the sugar, coconut, rolled oats and cornflakes in a large bowl.

In a small pan heat the butter and honey on a low heat and stir occasionally.

When completely melted remove and pour into the dry ingredients.

Mix thoroughly with a metal spoon.

Spoon the mixture into a lightly greased tray and bake for 30 minutes or until golden brown. Slice whilst still warm into diamonds.

The coconut is the fruit of the coconut palm which comprises of an outer fibrous husk containing an edible sweet, white flesh and cold coconut water.

The coconut palm is one of the most important crop trees in the world and each part of the tree has some value attached to it.

The most important product is the copra, which is the dried extracted kernal from which the oil is made. Copra is also used as a live stock feed, a fertiliser and to make the more widely known dessicated or shredded coconut.

Coir is made from the husk and is used to make ropes, baskets, brushes and mats. The flowering stalks of the palm are tapped and yield a sweet liquid which is sometimes fermented and distilled.

The young buds are eaten as a vegetable, the leaves are used for thatching and making baskets. The trunk is utilised in carpentry.

When the coconut is first harvested, the outer husk is green and the flesh is soft and the water sweet and refreshing. When it is ready to be used in the culinary world, the shell will have darkened, the flesh thickened and the water much reduced in volume.

Coconut is used to flavour and thicken curries as a filling for pies and as a flavouring for cakes and confectionary or even decorations.

It is very versatile, available in many forms, fresh, shredded or as a block in creamed coconut. Coconut milk is also available in a can and is often added to flavour and thicken curries.

When selecting a coconut, shake it to be certain you can hear the liquid within. If you can't then the coconut is dry and probably rotten inside.

Fig & Nut *Biscuits*

These delicious biscuits will make a tempting compliment to your cup of tea as well as providing good nutritional values.

Ingredients
225 g – 8 oz flour
1 tsp baking powder
1/4 tsp grated nutmeg
Pinch of salt
85 g – 3 oz butter
115 g – 4 oz soft brown sugar
1 egg – lightly beaten
1 tbsp double cream
8 dried figs, finely chopped
115 g – 4 oz lightly toasted, chopped
Pistachio nuts

Method
350°F – 180°C - Gas Mark 4

In a mixing bowl sift the flour, baking powder, nutmeg and salt. Slice the butter into small pieces and add to the mixture. Rub the butter between fingertips to resemble fine breadcrumbs.

With a wooden spoon, stir in the sugar, beaten egg and the cream.

Beat everything well together until it is smooth. Finally fold in the figs and nuts and mix thoroughly.

The mixture should now be stiff enough to roll out. You may need to add a little more flour if necessary.

On a lightly floured surface roll out the dough into 1/8th" thick.

Cut the dough into circles with a pastry cutter.

Knead and roll out the remaining dough until it is all used up. Place the circles on a greased baking sheet.

Bake for 10-15 minutes just above the centre of the pre heated oven until the biscuits are golden.

Remove the baking sheet from the oven and transfer onto a cooling tray.

European *Biscuits*

These biscuits are fairly European and carry the taste of the humble sesame seed.

Ingredients
175 g – 6 oz unsalted butter
175 g – 6 oz light brown sugar
85 g – 3 oz light golden syrup
1 egg
225 g – 8 oz plain flour
2 tsp baking powder
2 tbsp cocoa powder
1 tsp cinnamon powder-mixed
with 1 tsp raw cane sugar
200 g – 7 oz dark plain melted chocolate
200 g – 7 oz roasted sesame seeds

Method
350°F – 180°C - Gas Mark 4

Soften the butter and cream together with the sugar and syrup until light and fluffy.

Add the egg and whisk until well combined.

Sift flour, baking powder, cocoa and the cinnamon together and then add half to the mixture and mix. Then mix in the other half lightly and cover with a cling film and chill for an hour in the fridge.

Line baking sheets with baking paper and take walnut sized portions of the mixture and roll into balls.

Dip half of the bowl into the cinnamon - sugar and place on the prepared sheets.

Allow at least 2 inches between each biscuit for spreading then bake in the preheated oven for 12 minutes.

Remove and cool slightly on the sheet then transfer onto a cooling tray.

When they have cooled, dip the bases lightly in chocolate then in the sesame seeds.

Place on a cooling tray to set completely.

Oat *Crunchies*

The oats in this recipe make the biscuits really crunchy, don't forget the goodness they contain.

Ingredients
115 g – 4 oz butter
115 g – 4 oz margarine
175 g – 6 oz sugar
1 egg
250 g – 9 oz flour
1 tsp baking powder
5 tbsp rolled oats

Method
350˚F – 180˚C - Gas Mark 4

Cream the butter, margarine and sugar together until it is light and fluffy.

Beat in the egg gradually. Then add the sifted flour and baking powder and mix well together.

Using your hands lightly knead the mixture until it forms a smooth but stiff dough. Spread the oats onto a plate and divide the dough into 18 equal portions.

Roll each into a bowl then into the oats. Slightly flatten each ball then place well spaced apart onto a greased baking sheet in a fridge to chill for 30 minutes.   Bake in a pre heated oven for 25 minutes or until they are golden brown.

Allow to cool slightly before lifting off onto a cooling tray.

Orange *Biscuits*

These biscuits have a distinct orange flavour. They can be prepared ahead of time and left in the fridge or freezer for instant baking.

Ingredients
300 g – 10 oz plain flour
1 tsp baking powder
150 g – 5 oz butter
175 g – caster sugar
2 tsp finely grated orange rind
1 lightly beaten egg
55 g – 2 oz raisins
Caster sugar for sprinkling

Method
350˚F – 180˚C - Gas Mark 4

Sieve together the flour and baking powder. Cream together the butter, sugar and orange rind until light and fluffy.

Beat in the eggs and stir in the raisins and the flour until the mixture has all clung together. On a lightly floured surface, form into a roll about 2 inches - 5 cm thick.

Wrap in foil and chill in the fridge for a few hours.

When you want to bake them, slice thinly, sprinkle with caster sugar and bake on a greased baking tray for just 15 minutes in a pre heated oven.

Allow to cool on the sheets for a couple of minutes then transfer onto a cooling tray.

Chocolate *Pinwheels*

These pinwheels have a delicious combined flavour of chocolate as well as lemon and have been made larger then the average biscuit to define the wheels.

Ingredients
175 g – 6 oz softened butter
300 g – 10 oz caster sugar
1 well beaten egg
350 g – 12 oz plain flour
25 g – 1 oz dark, melted chocolate
Grated rind of a lemon

Method
375 °F – 190 °C - Gas Mark 5

In a large bowl, cream together the butter and sugar until light and fluffy.

Gradually add the beaten egg to the creamy mixture, beating well after each addition.

Sieve the flour into the creamed mixture and mix together until it forms a soft dough.

Transfer half of this mixture to another bowl and beat in the melted chocolate.

Stir the grated lemon rind into the other half. On a lightly floured surface roll out the two pieces of dough to form rectangles of the same size.

The bigger the roll the bigger the biscuit will be.

Lay the lemon dough on top of the chocolate dough and roll tightly into a swiss roll shape. Cover in cling film and chill in the fridge for an hour.

Meanwhile grease and flour a baking sheet.

After an hour cut with a sharp knife into 1/4 inch thick slices.

Bake on the sheets and bake in a pre heated oven for about 12 minutes or until lightly golden.

After a minute on the tray transfer the biscuits onto a cooling tray and allow to cool.

Lemon *Creams*

These are crisp and tangy biscuits, which are creamed together with lemon icing.

Ingredients
175 g – 6 oz butter
150 g – 5 oz caster sugar
1 egg yolk
1/4 tsp lemon essence
225 g – 8 oz self raising flour

Method
400 °F – 200 °C - Gas Mark 6

Cream together the butter and sugar with the essence.

When light and fluffy, stir in the egg yolks and lemon essence.

Add the flour, a little at a time and continue beating until the mixture forms firm dough.

On a floured surface roll out to 1/4" thick.

Using a 3" pastry cutter cut the dough and place them well spaced on a lightly greased baking sheet.

Bake for almost 12 minutes, when they should be lightly golden.

Remove onto a cooling tray and cool before serving.

Cream the biscuits together with mock icing which has been flavoured with a few drops of lemon essence.

Chocolate *Pinwheels*

Novelty *Wheels*

Irresistible and a good excuse for a cup of tea. Coloured sugar adds visual appeal if you can find some in specialist shops.

Ingredients
175 g – 6 oz plain flour
1/4 tsp salt
55 g – 2 oz sugar
1 tsp baking powder
55 g – 2 oz butter
Few drops vanilla
Milk to make dough
1 tsp cocoa powder

Method
350˚F – 180˚C - Gas Mark 4

Sift the flour, salt, sugar and baking powder. Rub in the butter and add the vanilla and coconut.

Mix well. Pour in enough milk to make a soft biscuit dough. Divide into two. In one half mix the sifted cocoa powder. Roll out both pieces of dough into an oblong shape, then place the chocolate flavoured dough onto the other one.

Roll into a large Swiss roll shape.

Cover with cling film and place in the fridge for an hour to chill.

Lightly grease a baking sheet and then slice the roll sharply into 1/4" slices.

Sprinkle coloured sugar granules over the top if available and place on the sheet and bake in a pre heated oven.

After about 15 - 20 minutes, remove from the oven and cool on the tray for a few minutes before transferring onto a cooling tray.

Nutty *Wonders*

These are one of my favourite recipes, the taste is sensational.

Ingredients
175 g – 6 oz butter
85 g – 3 oz sugar
2 eggs
375 g – 13 oz plain flour
1 tsp baking powder
1/2 tsp bicarbonate of soda
150 g – 5 oz chopped nuts
85 g – 3 oz chopped dates

Method
375˚F – 190˚C - Gas Mark 5

In a large mixing bowl, cream together the butter and sugar.

Beat well together then add the beaten eggs slowly beating well again.

Mix together the sifted dry ingredients, nuts and the dates and knead everything together. Make small balls, as they will expand a lot and flatten very slightly.

Bake in small batches in a pre heated oven for about 25 minutes. Cool on a wire tray.

Nutty *Slices*

When set cut into slices with a hot knife and drizzle over with extra chocolate.

Ingredients

225 g – 8 oz caster sugar
2 tbsp golden syrup
115 g – 4 oz unsalted butter
115 g – 4 oz liquid glucose
410 g – 13 oz sweetened condensed milk
1 tbsp instant coffee granules dissolved
in 3 fl oz hot water
300 g – 10 oz chopped walnuts or pecan nuts
350 g – 12 oz plain or semi sweet melted chocolate

Method

In a large heavy based pan, mix together the golden syrup, sugar, butter, glucose and condensed milk. Stir continuously and slowly allow the mixture to come to the boil. Continue boiling the mixture until it becomes thick and a light golden brown colour. Keep stirring at all times to avoid sticking. Add the coffee mixture and nuts.

Remove saucepan from the heat and pour the mixture into a lightly greased baking sheet. Refrigerate until firm or overnight if possible.

When firm cut into 6 strips, cutting right across the baking sheet.

Drizzle the melted chocolate over and allow to set.

The supermarket shelves are overflowing with a wonderful array of nuts, dates and fresh and dried fruits of every kind, from every country and continent.

We are so used to the traditional almonds and pistachio nuts that we use the other nuts only occasionally.

But why? Have you seen what nature has to offer us, and packed with nutritional values?

We must include them in our diets.

Hazelnuts, Pecan nuts, Walnuts, Brazil nuts, Chestnuts, Pine nuts, and many more.

Moreover, they all contain valuable vitamins and boost your energy.

The actual term 'nut' is used to describe the seed. Basically it's a fruit with an edible kernel inside the hard shell.

Shelled, flaked or groundnuts are best bought in small quantities for freshness.

Surprisingly they are best stored in glass containers and in the fridge. Nuts such as Brazil nuts or pecan nuts should feel heavy when bought. If they are light they are probably all dried up inside and not worth paying for. It is important that the nuts are bought as fresh as possible and in smaller quantities as they do turn rancid in time. You will find the flavours of the nuts are more pronounced when they are roasted. Pale coloured almonds look especially attractive when sliced and lightly toasted to give a pinkish tinge. You can buy the ground and powdered forms but nuts ground at home will give the freshness, flavour and deeper aroma then commercially groundnuts.

Nuts used in baking or cooking or even decoration can add that crunch and appeal, tinged with different colours such as light green or rose pink can give an amazing finish.

Choc Chip *Biscuits*

These biscuits are a favourite with children and the addition of walnuts makes them really special.

Ingredients
115 g – 4 oz butter
115 g – 4 oz granulated sugar
85 g – 3 oz brown sugar
1 beaten egg
1 tsp vanilla essence
175 g – 6 oz self raising flour
1/2 tsp salt
1/2 tsp bicarbonate of soda
55 g – 2 oz chopped walnuts
115 g – 4 oz chocolate chips

Method
375 °F - 190 °C - Gas Mark 5

In a mixing bowl cream the butter, then gradually add the two sugars until very light and frothy. Add the beaten egg, beating all the time then finally add the vanilla essence.

Sift the flour, salt and soda into the mixture and fold in with a metal spoon. When mixed thoroughly add the walnuts and chocolate chips, combine well.

On a lightly greased baking sheet, drop teaspoons of this mixture spacing the biscuits an inch apart. Bake in the pre heated oven for almost 12 minutes or until cooked. Cool on a wire tray.

Allow to cool and store in an airtight tin.

Easy *Chocolate Slices*

A crisp biscuit and chocolate cake. Simple to make, cut into slices and serve chilled.

Ingredients
250 g – 9 oz plain chocolate
280 ml – 10 fl oz tub of double cream
2 tsp vanilla essence
15 Nice biscuits

Method
Break the chocolate into rough chunks. Heat the cream in a pan over a low heat until almost boiling then add the chocolate and remove from the heat.

Cover the pan for about 5 minutes, then add the vanilla essence to the mixture and begin stirring until smooth.

Pour the mixture into a large bowl and chill until it begins to thicken. Line a 450 g - 1 lb loaf tin with cling film overlapping the edges of the tin.

Spread 1/6th of the chocolate mixture over the base of the tin. Cover with a layer of biscuits then repeat in this fashion until the last layer is of the chocolate.

Cover with the cling film then chill for a few hours until the chocolate has set firmly.

Unwrap the cling film from the top of the cake and turn out onto a serving plate.

Carefully peel of the cling film and slice thinly and serve.

***Tip: Digestive biscuits will give a crunchier texture, but crush into coarse crumbs first.**

Viennese *Whirls*

A popular and easy biscuit to make, make it different each time by sprinkling assorted decorations or even drizzling chocolate over them.

Ingredients
225 g – 8 oz marg
85 g – 3 oz icing sugar
Few drops of vanilla essence
200 g – 7 oz self raising flour
55 g – 2 oz corn flour

Method
350°F – 180°C - Gas Mark 4

Cream together the margarine and sugar until very pale in colour. Add the vanilla and cream again. Sift the flour and corn flour twice then fold in gently into the creamed mixture. Fit a piping bag with a 1/2 inch nozzle then fill with cream. Place bun cases in a 16 hole bun tin and pipe the mixture into a circle around the base of the case. In a preheated oven bake for almost 25 minutes until light golden in colour.

Cool completely when baked then sandwich together with red jam and dredge with icing sugar.

Papaya *Biscuits*

These really are my favourite biscuits, no matter how many you bake they always seem to finish very quickly.

Ingredients
225 g – 8 oz butter
175 g – 6 oz caster sugar
1 beaten egg
175 g – 6 oz plain flour
2 tsp baking powder
115 g – 4 oz wholemeal flour
175 g – 6 oz dried, chopped papaya
175 g – 6 oz sweetened shredded coconut
2 limes

Method
375°F – 190°C - Gas Mark 5

Using an electric blender beat together the butter and sugar until soft and light.

Beat in the egg gradually then fold in the sifted plain flour and baking powder.

Grate the rind of the limes and add to the mixture with the remaining ingredients.

Roll the dough into small walnut sized balls with floured hands. Place on lightly greased baking sheets and allow enough space between them, as they will spread out.

Bake in a preheated oven for 15 minutes until golden.

Cool slightly before transferring to a cooling tray.

Papayas vary enormously in appearance and type. There are orange and green varieties which can vary greatly in size. Some are small enough for one person to manage. These are the kind we see in our supermarkets and local corner grocers.

Others are enough for the family.

The papaya is a giant plant rather than a tree. When the fruit is formed it grows close under the tree and down the stem in a great cluster.

The fruit makes a perfect breakfast in the tropics, where you can eat beautifully cut apricot-pink slices accompanied by a wedge of lime or two.

Lime is an essential partner for papaya-as it is for a number of other mild tropical fruits.

To prepare the fruit, halve it and scrape out the deep grey seeds. Peel and use as required. The succulent flesh is some what watery, pink or orange in colour and encloses a central mass of seeds.

Dried papaya can be used in many ways, but here it's used as the main ingredient in biscuits.

Date *Slices*

Hard to believe that such tempting slices can be made in a very short time, using everyday ingredients.

Ingredients
225 g – chopped dates
225 g – 8 oz softened butter
6 fl oz water
115 g – 4 oz rolled oats
150 g – 5 oz wholemeal flour
2 tbsp clear honey
1/2 tsp allspice

Method
350°F – 180°C - Gas Mark 4

In a small saucepan, simmer the dates in the water until the dates are soft.

Mash together with a fork until it's like a pulp then cool completely.

In a medium sized bowl, put the oats, the sifted flour and butter.

Using your finger tips rub the butter until it resembles coarse fine bread crumbs.

Prepare a 20 cm - 8 inch shallow cake tin by greasing it lightly with melted butter.

Divide the mixture into two and press down half of the mixture evenly and firmly into the tin.

Combine the honey and spice with the date pulp and spread evenly over the mixture already in the tin.

Spread the remaining half of the mixture and press down firmly before baking in the pre heated oven.

After almost 25-30 minutes take out of the oven and cut into sharp slices. They will be soft and crumbly whilst still hot but when cooled will harden slightly as the mixture sets.

Light *Biscuits*

A delicious biscuit and very dainty looking with the softening effect of the dusted icing sugar.

Ingredients
115 g – 4 oz marg
115 g – 4 oz caster sugar
1 egg yolk
Few drops of vanilla essence
225 g – 8 oz plain flour
2 tsp sour cream
2 tsp strawberry jam
2 tsp apricot jam
Icing sugar

Method
350°F – 180°C - Gas Mark 4

Cream margarine and sugar, then beat in the egg yolk and vanilla essence.

Blend in the flour to form a soft dough.

Turn out onto a lightly floured board and roll into 1/8th thickness.

Using a fluted round cutter, cut 12 circles.

Place on a lightly greased baking sheet and bake in a pre heated oven for almost 20 mins or until golden brown.

Dust with icing sugar when baked and cool completely.

Trifle *Fingers*

These biscuits are really easy to make and can be stored in an airtight container. Ideal for using as a layer for trifles and fruit custards.

Ingredients
1 tsp butter
85 g – 3 oz + 2 tsp plain flour
115 g – 4 oz + 2 tsp caster sugar
4 eggs separated
Few drops almond essence

Method
350°F – 180°C - Gas Mark 4

Grease two baking sheets with butter, and sprinkle the 2 tsp of flour over the baking sheets.

In a large bowl, combine the 115 g - 4 oz of sugar, egg yolks and the essence and beat till thick and pale in colour.

Using a metal spoon, fold in the remaining flour and mix well.

In a separate bowl, beat the egg whites until they form peaks.

Fold this into the mixture gently and spoon half of the batter into a large piping back fitted with a 1/2" plain nozzle.

Pipe 3" lengths onto the baking sheet.

Sprinkle remaining sugar over the shapes and bake in a pre heated oven for 12 minutes or until light and firm to the touch.

Cool completely and store and use as required.

Red Cherry *Biscuits*

These light biscuits are delicious as well as attractive with the addition of halved, glaced cherries.

Ingredients
175 g – 6 oz softened butter
55 g – 2 oz caster sugar
175 g – 6 oz plain flour
55 g – 2 oz corn flour
115 g – 4 oz halved glaced cherries
Coloured desiccated coconut for sprinkling

Method
350°F – 175°C - Gas Mark 4

In a large mixing bowl beat the butter and sugar until it is light and fluffy.

Rinse the cherries to take away the syrup, which will make them heavy, and dry on a kitchen towel. Stir into the flour and form into a roll.

Cover well with cling film then chill for an hour in the refrigerator.

Lightly grease two baking sheets with vegetable oil.

Take out the roll, which should be cold and firm now and cut into 5mm - 1/2" slices.

Place them all on the baking sheets and sprinkle with coloured coconut, slightly pressing into the biscuits.

Bake in a pre heated oven for 20 minutes until lightly brown.

Allow 5 minutes on the baking sheet before transferring onto the cooling tray.

Store in an airtight container.

***Tip: make these biscuits look different each time by adding different colours of cherries.**

Red Cherry *Biscuits*

Sesame Seed *Slices*

These slices are very tasty and so nutritious, look at the ingredients and see how simple and easy the method is.

Ingredients
200 g – 7 oz rolled oats
85 g – 3 oz sesame seeds
200 g – 7 oz soft brown sugar
Pinch of salt
150 g – 5 oz desiccated coconut
225 g – 8 oz melted butter

Method
375˚F – 190˚C - Gas Mark 5

In a mixing bowl, combine all the dry ingredients.

Then pour in the melted butter and mix well together until everything is thoroughly mixed.

Spoon the mixture into a lightly greased 20 cm - 8" tin and smooth the top with the back of a metal spoon.

Place the tin in a pre heated oven. Bake for 30 minutes until the mixture is bubbling at the edges.

Remove from the oven and set aside to cool completely.

With a sharp knife cut into slices and serve.

A man returns very ill from Africa. He goes to see his doctor, and is immediately rushed to the hospital to undergo a barrage of tests. The man wakes up after the tests in a private room at the hospital, and the phone by his bed rings. "This is your doctor. We've had the results back from your tests and we've found you have a nasty virus, which is extremely contagious!"

"Oh no," groaned the man, "What are you going to do, doctor?"

"Well we're going to put you on a diet of sesame slices, pancakes, and pitta bread."

"Oh thank goodness, and that will cure me completely?" the man asked with a sigh of relief.

The doctor replied, "Well no, not exactly but for the moment it's the only food we can get under the door."

Star *Biscuits*

These biscuits can be made to look different each time by sprinkle decorations of your choice.

Ingredients
225 g – 8 oz butter
115 g – 4 oz caster sugar
1/2 tsp almond essence
1/4 tsp vanilla essence
2 egg yolks
300 g – 10 oz self raising flour
Pinch of salt
Ground pistachio nuts for decoration.

Method
375˚F – 190˚C - Gas Mark 5

Beat together the butter until light and fluffy

then stir in the sugar, almond and vanilla essence.

Beat again until light and fluffy.

Beat in the egg yolks until they are thoroughly combined.

Sift the flour and salt into the mixture then fold in the sifted flour.

Make sure the ingredients are well mixed.

Spoon the mixture into a large forcing bag, and using a 1/4" star nozzle pipe out some stars, onto a greased baking sheet.

Sprinkle with the ground pistachio nuts.

Bake in a pre heated oven and bake for 10-15 minutes.

Cool on a wire tray when baked and lightly golden.

Traditional *Coconut Biscuits*

*Biscuits with a delicious coconut crunch taste.
I usually allow them to over brown slightly for
an even better taste.*

Ingredients
225 g – 8 oz butter
225 g – 8 oz sugar
3 eggs
Few drops vanilla essence
450 g – 1 lb plain flour
3 tsp baking powder
85 g – 3 oz desiccated coconut

Method
375 °F – 190 °C - Gas Mark 5

Cream together the butter and sugar in a
mixing bowl. In a smaller bowl beat together
the eggs with the vanilla. Slowly beat the
eggs into the creamed mixture until it has all
been used up.

Fold in the sifted flour and baking powder,
then finally the coconut.

Mix well together lightly, until it has
formed a soft biscuit dough.

Using a biscuit maker, press out into
required shapes onto a baking sheet.
Alternatively roll out onto a lightly floured
board and cut into attractive shapes.
Decorate with coloured coconut or any
other decoration.

Bake for almost 20 minutes or until a light
golden shade and cool on a wire tray.

Treacle *Nut Biscuits*

*A special taste and richer appearance with the
addition of treacle.*

Ingredients
175 g – 6 oz softened butter
200 g – 7 oz light brown sugar
3 tbsp treacle
1 beaten egg
250 g – 9 oz plain flour
1 tsp baking powder
1 tsp grated nutmeg
1 tsp salt
115 g – 4 oz chopped hazel nuts

Method
350 °F – 180 °C - Gas Mark 4

In a mixing bowl beat the sugar and butter
until light and fluffy.

Gradually beat in the treacle and egg which
has been previously whisked together with
an electric beater.

Sift in the flour, baking powder, nutmeg
and salt.

Mix well together. Fold in the hazelnuts
and form into a dough.

Wrap in cling film and chill in a refrigerator
for a few hours.

Lightly grease two baking sheets with
vegetable oil.

Taking a teaspoon of the dough, form into
a round ball then flatten slightly.

Fill the baking sheet up with these
circles and bake in a pre heated oven for
20 minutes.

Remove from the oven then cool for a few
minutes before transferring onto a
cooling rack.

Biscuits & Slices

Ginger *Slices*

These ginger slices are as delicious as they are nutritious.

Ingredients
225 g – 8 oz ghee
450 g – 1 lb jaggery
225 g – 8 oz ginger
115 g – 4 oz ground almonds
175 g – 6 oz desiccated coconut
55 g – 2 oz poppy seeds

Decoration
85 g – 3 oz sliced fresh coconut
1 tbsp roasted sesame seeds
1 tbsp ground pistachio nuts

Method
Wash, peel and finely grate the ginger. In a large pan, warm the ghee and jaggery on a medium heat until melted.

Add the prepared ginger and braise very slowly until slightly browned and almost dry in texture.

Mix in all the other ingredients and continue to stir for the next 15 minutes on the lowest setting. After this time turn out into a greased baking tray.

Mark into squares or diamonds and decorate. Allow to set before serving.

The hakims in India often sell recipes for palatable herbs which help towards the recovery and prevention from certain ailments.

Some of these recipes have acquired the status of family heirlooms.

The creation of these specialities seem to be a dying art as the modern trend seems to be to take mixture and capsules to ward of colds and coughs, rather then the natural methods.

Ginger is universally recognised as an effective root vegetable in medicine. It's powers are enormous and in the East, dry golden, aromatic ginger is used for relieving muscular aches and pains by rubbing the powder on the body. Internally it is taken as a digestive and the hakims advise that at the onset of winter, chopped ginger should be added to your tea.

Ginger slices are extremely nourishing as they contain ingredients high in iron and vitamins. The amount of ginger used here can be varied according to preference and the strength of the ginger. It is given in the mildest form acceptable to all ages.

Hazelnut *Biscuits*

These are traditional European biscuits which are often served with desserts.

Ingredients
225 g – 8 oz butter
225 g – 8 oz sugar
1 lightly beaten egg
1 tsp vanilla essence
Pinch of nutmeg powder
300 g – 10 oz self raising flour
1/2 tsp baking powder
85 g – 3 oz ground hazelnuts
1 tbsp icing sugar

Method
350˚F – 180˚C - Gas Mark 4

In a large mixing bowl cream the butter and sugar until it's light and fluffy. Then beat in the egg, vanilla essence and the nutmeg.

Sift in the rest of the ingredients apart from the icing sugar. Fold with a metal spoon and mix well together.

Fit a large piping bag with a 1/2" nozzle and pipe into spirals on a greased baking sheet. Bake in the pre heated oven until just turning golden then cool slightly.

Transfer onto a cooling tray and dust with the icing sugar.

Walnut *Diamonds*

These are delicious diamonds with a date and walnut topping.

Ingredients

115 g – 4 oz butter
115 g – 4 oz caster sugar
2 egg yolks
1/2 tsp vanilla essence
225 g – 8 oz self raising flour

Topping

3 tbsp apricot jam
1 tsp lemon juice
2 egg whites
1 tbsp caster sugar
55 g – 2 oz finely chopped dates
55 g – 2 oz finely chopped walnuts
1 tsp grated orange rind

Method

350°F – 180°C - Gas Mark 4

Cream the butter and sugar together with a wooden spoon until very light and fluffy. Beat in the yolks and vanilla essence.

Add the sifted flour and stir well, mixing everything well together.

Turn the mixture into a 20 cm - 8" square baking tin and press down firmly.

Prick all over with a fork and bake in a pre heated oven for 10 minutes.

By now the edges should have just begun to turn golden brown.

In a small glass bowl mix the jam and lemon juice together. When the tray has been removed from the oven, brush with this jam and lemon juice mixture.

In a medium sized bowl beat the egg whites until soft peaks are formed.

Add the sugar and beat until stiff again.

Gently fold in the dates, walnuts and orange rind with a metal spoon.

Pile this on top of the jam-glazed biscuits and spread out evenly using a spatula.

Return to the oven and bake for another 15 minutes.

The meringue should have turned a beautiful light, golden shade and be firm to the touch. After the mixture has cooled cut into diamond shapes.

Walnut *Wonders*

These biscuits are simply divine, bringing instant warmth on a cold winter's day.

Ingredients

175 g – 6 oz butter
175 g – 6 oz sugar
2 eggs
Few drops vanilla essence
375 g – 13 oz plain flour
1/2 tsp bicarbonate of soda
1 tsp baking powder
115 g – 4 oz chopped walnuts
115 g – 4 oz chopped dates
Extra flour if needed to make a pliable dough
Crushed cornflakes

Method

375°F – 190°C - Gas Mark 5

With an electric mixer, cream together the butter and sugar.

Beat the eggs and vanilla essence until light and frothy.

Into the bowl sift the flour, bicarbonate of soda and baking powder.

Add all the other ingredients except the cornflakes.

Mix well together with your hands. The dough should be firm but a little sticky. Add as much extra flour as necessary. If it is too dry you may need to add a little milk to make it slightly sticky.

Make small balls between your palms and flatten very slightly.

Roll this into the crushed cornflakes and place evenly and well spaced onto a baking tray. Bake in a preheated oven or until lightly golden.

Allow to cool in the tray for a while then remove onto the cooling tray.

Honey *Biscuits*

Oil is the substitute for butter and honey is the key ingredient. You really have to bake and taste these biscuits to appreciate the nutritional values.

Ingredients
125 g – 5 oz butter
2 tsp finely grated lemon rind
85 g – 3 oz caster sugar
80 ml – 3 fl oz vegetable oil
300 g – 10 oz plain flour
150 g – 5 oz self raising flour
25 g – 1 oz finely chopped walnuts

Glace
160 ml – 6 fl oz orange juice
250 ml – 9 fl oz clear honey
2 tsp ground pistachio

Method
350°F – 180°C - Gas Mark 4

With an electric mixture beat together the butter, rind and sugar.

Gradually beat in the oil until the mixture is really light and fluffy.

Stir in the sifted flours, nuts and enough juice to make a soft pliable dough. Take a table spoon of the mixture and shape into oval shapes. Flatten slightly with the back of a fork and place on a greased baking tray. Continue doing this to the rest of the dough then bake in a pre heated oven.

When lightly golden take out and lift onto a cooling tray.

For the glaze heat the honey in a small microwave bowl or a pan. Dip the cooled biscuits individually into the honey and then sprinkle with the sesame seeds and the ground pistachio nuts.

Honey Nut *Diamonds*

These honey nut diamonds are very healthy and nutritional enough to eat at any time of the day.

Ingredients
175 g – 6 oz set honey
175 g – 6 oz butter
85 g – 3 oz caster sugar
115 g – 4 oz dried apricots
1 tsp baking powder
225 g – 8 oz self raising flour
2 beaten eggs
25 g – 1 oz flaked almonds
25 g – 1 oz ground pistachio
25 g – 1 oz poppy seeds

Method
160°C – 325°F - Gas Mark 3

In a heavy based saucepan melt the sugar, butter and honey, then add the apricots which have been cut into small pieces.

Allow to cool slightly then beat in the eggs.

Sift in the flour and baking powder then transfer into a square lightly greased tin.

Sprinkle the almonds, pistachio and poppy seeds and bake in a pre heated oven for around 45 minutes until well risen and golden.

Allow to cool slightly then using a sharp knife cut into diamond shapes.

Cornflake *Biscuits*

These small chocolate biscuits are filled with cornflakes then dusted with icing sugar or drinking chocolate. You can make them larger, sandwich together with strawberries and cream for a really special treat.

Ingredients
210 g – 7 oz unsalted butter
115 g – 4 oz brown sugar
1 beaten egg
225 g – 8 oz plain flour
4 tbsp cocoa powder
2 tsp baking powder
55 g – 2 oz desiccated coconut
85 g – 3 oz Cornflakes
Drinking chocolate or icing sugar for dusting

Method
350˚F – 180˚C - Gas Mark 4

Beat the butter and sugar together, in a mixing bowl until light and fluffy.

Add the egg and mix until well combined then sift the flour, cocoa powder and the baking powder and mix by hand.

Lastly add the coconut and cornflakes and mix very lightly until well combined.

Place heaped teaspoonfuls of mixture onto two greased and lined baking sheets then bake for 12 minutes. Cool on the sheets and dust with the sifted icing sugar or cocoa powder just before serving.

Nest *Biscuits*

Easy to make and extremely delicious and tempting.

Ingredients
115 g – 4 oz butter
55 g – 2 oz caster sugar
1 egg
200 g – 7 oz self raising flour
Pinch of salt
Coconut

Method
350F – 180C - Gas Mark 4

Cream the butter with the sugar until light and creamy.

Separate the egg and beat in the yolk then mix all the dry ingredients together.

Take a small piece of the dough and roll into a ball.

Continue doing this and then dip these balls into the beaten egg white.

Make a small dent in the middle and roll in the coconut.

Fill the dent in the centre with the jam and then bake for almost 20 mins. Cool on a tray.

*** Tip: Roll in ground almonds to get a richer flavour**

Sweets & Desserts

Coconut Ice Cream **p84**

Almond *Helwa*

This helwa is enjoyable to make as well as to eat. The pleasure is in knowing that you made it yourself.

Ingredients
115 g – 4 oz cornflour
175 g – 6 oz flaked almonds
3 tbsp ghee - clarified butter
Few drops food colouring of your choice

Optional – cardammon powder

Syrup
2.5 pt water
22 oz – 1.5 lb sugar
(to make a thick, not sugary syrup)

Method
350˚F – 180˚C - Gas mark 4

In a saucepan, boil the syrup as described.

Whisk the corn flour with the remaining water then boil together in a large heavy pan, stirring all the time.

When the cornflour mixture has thickened, add the syrup which should be ready and the almonds, then keep boiling over a moderate heat until it is thick and slippery.

Add the ghee to this, then the colour and cardammon if required.

Grease a shallow baking tray and pour the mixture into this. Spread evenly and bake in a pre heated oven. After 20 minutes take out and whilst still warm slice.

It is a fact of life that Asian sweets and desserts are incredibly high in calories.

But the syrup and sugar laced temptations are synonymous with festivity and jubilation. Thankfully they are not eaten every day.

Sitting in a marquee, with friends a few days before a wedding, everyone seemed to be discussing how much weight they were piling on.

The group of women all nodded in agreement acknowledging the high calories and sugary contents of certain sweets, and agreeing that we should be more conscious of what we ate.

This teamed with sufficient exercise would be the perfect solution for losing weight, becoming more fit and active and have a general feeling of well being.

It was agreed upon that it wasn't really necessary to consume as much sugar as we did. Some of us blamed it on hereditary whilst others were happy to admit having a sweet tooth. The welcome comment, "oh, well, we only live once so we might as well make the most of it." This brought much laughter and comfort to those who were pre occupied with dietary worries.

Along with thoughts and resolutions, and the momentarily promise of self-education in health, exercising and correct diet soon went flying into thin air as the trays of sweets were passed around at that moment.

Laden with guilt and mischief each person reached out to the tempting array of helwa's, biscuits and sweets, probably thought in their mind, that the diet would start tomorrow. But forget that and concentrate on the Helwa itself.

The end result will make you wonder why you never discovered it before.

Try it! Forget the calories for once, like they said the diet can start tomorrow.

Apple *Pudding*

Make good use of the English cooking apples and serve this pudding with single cream or hot custard.

Ingredients
55 g – 2 oz softened butter
85 g – 3 oz caster sugar
3 well beaten eggs
115 g – 4 oz sifted self raising flour
2 cooking apples, peeled, cored and sliced
55 g – 2 oz raisins

Topping
85 g – 3 oz self raising flour
1/2 tsp cinnamon powder
40 g – 1.5 oz butter
25 g – 1 oz caster sugar

Decoration
1 red dessert apple-thinly sliced and tossed in lemon juice
2 tbsp sifted caster sugar
Pinch of ground cinnamon

Method

350°F – 180°C - Gas Mark 4

Make the base by beating together the butter, sugar, eggs and flour for 2 minutes until smooth.

Spoon into a prepared 18cm spring form tin, which has been lined with greased paper. Mix together the sliced apples and raisins and spread evenly over the top. Then make the topping by sifting the flour and cinnamon together.

Rub in the butter into the flour until it resembles fine breadcrumbs and then stir in the sugar. Sprinkle this over the apples and raisins evenly.

Bake in a centre of the oven about an hour. Remove from the oven and cool for 10 minutes in the tin before transferring onto a cooling tray and peeling of the paper.

Decorate and serve warm or cold with custard and cream.

Apricot *Treats*

Apricot treats are really easy to make, and taste delicious with that certain edge to it, camaflaged with the sweetness of the muscavado sugar.

Ingredients
175 g – 6 oz dried apricots - pureed
55 g – 2 oz unsalted butter, melted
2 fl oz water
225 g – 8 oz light muscavado sugar
1 tsp lemon juice
2 fl oz single cream

Coating
Light muscavado sugar or desiccated coconut

Method

Wash and dry the apricots then chop very finely.

To the melted butter add the water, sugar and lemon juice in a non stick pan.

Heat until the sugar has dissolved completely, stirring all the time.

Boil until the mixture has reached the soft ball stage. Remove the pan from the heat and add the apricots, stir well and allow to cool completely.

Form into small balls then roll into the coating you prefer and fill the petit four cases.

Baklava

Baklava is a traditional Turkish sweet made from pastry and filled with a healthy and nutritious combination of nuts.

Ingredients

175 g – 6 oz ground pistachio nuts
175 g – 6 oz ground almonds
150 g – 5 oz icing sugar
1 tbsp ground cardammon
150 g – 5 oz unsalted melted butter
450 g – 1 lb filo pastry

Syrup
450 g – 1 lb granulated sugar
300 ml – 1/2 pt water
3 tbsp rose water

Method

325°F – 160°C - Gas Mark 3

Make the syrup first by boiling the sugar and water together. When it's reached the boiling point, simmer together until it is a medium consistency. Stir in the rose water and allow to cool.

In a medium sized bowl, mix together the nuts, icing sugar and cardammon powder.

Brush a large rectangular baking sheet with a little melted butter.

Take one sheet of filo pastry, remembering to keep the other sheets covered with a damp cloth to prevent drying out. Brush with melted butter and layer the baking sheet. Continue doing this until you have 6 sheets on top of each other and all buttered. Spread half of the nut mixture, press down lightly with the back of a metal spoon. Take another 6 sheets of filo pastry and butter in the same way.

Covering the nut mixture. Sprinkle the remaining mixture over these sheets and then layer with a final layer of 6 filo sheets brushed with butter.

Cut the pastry into sharp diamond shapes using a sharp knife.

Pour the remaining melted butter over the top. Bake for 20 minutes in the pre heated oven. After that time increase the heat to 200°C - 400°F - Gas Mark 6.

Bake for another 15 minutes until light shade of golden and slightly risen.

Remove from the oven and drizzle about 3/4 of the syrup over the top whilst still warm. Serve on a plate and when serving drizzle the extra syrup over the top for a sweeter and richer taste.

One day an eminent Hodja, a Turkish leader, was invited for a feast. He was very hungry and he finished all the specially prepared food that was presented before him. But, the host insisted he ate more. "Please Hodja eat some more food." Hodja declined putting up his hand, "no thanks! I am so full that, I can't have another morsel."

Then the servant came carrying a tray of baklava. The Hodja immediately reached out and started eating the baklava with haste enjoying each mouthful. The host commented politely "Hodja I'm very surprised! A couple of minutes ago you said that it was impossible for you to have another morsel. But now see that you have enough space in you stomach to swallow many slices of baklava." The Hodja replied smiling, "well you're right in your observation, but, I was right too. You see baklava is the Sultan of food. When it enters my stomach I am sure that some of the food I ate earlier will rise with respect and make place for the baklava."

Baklava

Date *Dessert*

A nomadic light and easy to prepare dessert. Made extensively in the Middle East and in Ramadan when dates are plentiful.

Ingredients
450 g – 1 lb stoned, dates
4 tangerines, peeled
12 fl oz single cream
25 g – 1 oz grated plain chocolate or
1 flake chocolate

Method
Prepare the fruit by chopping the dates into small pieces, slicing the bananas thinly and separating the tangerines into sections.

In a medium sized glass bowl, arrange some of the banana slices then pour about 2 fl oz of the cream over the top.

Then some of the dates followed by the cream and a portion of tangerines.

Continue in this fashion until all the fruit has been used up and the last of the cream is on top of the fruit. Cover with cling film and refrigerate for an hour.

Just before serving sprinkle with grated chocolate or a crumbled flake chocolate.

Turkish *Delight*

The ever popular Turkish delight, change the colouring and flavouring to make it different each time.

Ingredients
25 g – 1 oz gelatine
1/2 pt hot water
450 g – 1 lb caster sugar
1/4 tsp citric acid
1 tbsp rosewater
Few drops rose pink clouring
55 g – 2 oz icing sugar

Method
Sprinkle the gelatine over the hot water and stir until it has dissolved completely.

Pour this into a saucepan, then add the sugar and citric acid.

Stir over a low heat until the sugar has dissolved completely. Boil gently stirring occasionally for about 20 minutes.

Remove from the heat and stir in the rose water. Whisk the mixture lightly until it gives a sort of milky appearance.

Pour half of this mixture into a well greased square tin. Put this tin into another larger tin filled with cold water. This will cool the mixture almost immediately.

To the remaining half of the mixture add the food colouring and tint it.

Whisk lightly then spread over the first layer.

Cover with cling film and chill in the fridge.

Take a sheet of greaseproof paper and sift some icing sugar onto it. Turn out the Turkish delight onto that and cut into squares with a sharp knife or scissors. Coat well with some more of the icing sugar. Store in a plastic container or a tin and sprinkle more sugar over the top.

**TIP: Coat with toasted coconut, or chocolate strands to make it even more special.

Coconut *Fudge*

A delightful milk and coconut fudge decorated with tinted coconut, ground or slivered almonds, or even melted chocolate.

Ingredients
1 tsp softened butter
2 pts milk
115 g – 4 oz freshly grated coconut or dessicated coconut
115 g – 4 oz sugar
Few drops food colour - rose pink or yellow
1 tsp cardammon powder

Method

In a large heavy based saucepan. Boil the milk on a medium heat slowly.

Meanwhile grease a 20 cm - 8" shallow dish with the butter.

When the milk is bubbling increase the heat to a fairly high and boil briskly, stirring constantly.

The milk has to thicken until the point of setting. This takes time and patience and by no account must the milk be allowed to burn or the taste of the fudge will be completely spoilt. When the milk is reduced by almost half its original volume, after almost 45 minutes add the coconut and reduce the heat to low and continue stirring all the time for about another 10 minutes until it is very thick consistency.

Stir in the cardammon powder and the colouring of your choice and with a spatula ease out onto the dish and flatten until the top is even.

Decorate as you like and when cold cut into diamonds with a sharp knife.

Coconut *Marshmallows*

A little different method to Marshmallow Square's, but equally delicious. Marshmallows may take a few attempts before you get them exactly as you like.

Ingredients
4 tsp gelatine
9 fl oz hot water
375 g – 13 oz caster sugar
1 tsp vanilla essence
85 g – 3 oz desiccated coconut, toasted

Method
Sprinkle the gelatine in the hot water, then pour into a large bowl.

Add the sugar and essence and stir until the sugar has dissolved completely.

Whisk vigorously until the mixture has become very white and almost milky in appearance. It should have doubled in volume too.

The longer you beat the mixture the lighter it will be.

When the beating has thickened considerably, pour into a well greased square baking tin. Cover with cling film and chill for a few hours.

After this time cut into squares and roll in toasted coconut.

Date *Helawi*

Have fun making this helawi with children. It's a simple and enjoyable experience. Here I've doubled the recipe, as there never seems to be enough.

Ingredients

280 g – 10 oz butter
280 g – 10 oz sugar
2 eggs
1 large packet of Rich Tea or Marie biscuits
450 g – 1 lb dates (stoned)- packaged ones will suffice
115 g – 4 oz desiccated coconut
225 g – 8 oz chopped, toasted mixed nuts (walnuts, almonds, pistachio, hazel nuts or pecan nuts)

....

Method

Break the biscuits into rough pieces about quarter of the original size. Chop the dates very finely.

Melt the butter and sugar in a pan on a medium heat. Keep stirring until the sugar has dissolved and the butter has melted completely.

Add the dates to this and simmer slowly until they have softened. Remove from the heat and quickly add the well-beaten eggs. Beat into the mixture. Return to the stove and add the biscuits. Save a little of the nuts and coconut and add the remaining into the mixture.

Cook gently for a few minutes until all the ingredients are well mixed.

Turn out on to foil and shape into a roll. Sprinkle with remaining nuts and coconut then wrap in foil. Chill for a few hours before slicing thinly with a sharp knife.

Fig *Sweets*

These little sweets contain no added sugars. The figs should contain enough sweetness. Try them for after dinner sweets.

Ingredients

350 g – 12 oz dried figs
115 g – 4 oz dates
25 whole toasted almonds
85 g – 3 oz hazelnuts finely chopped
55 g – 2 oz almonds chopped
55 g – 2 oz pistachio nuts, chopped

....

Method

Chop the figs and dates and puree in a blender and transfer into a mixing bowl.

Shape this mixture into 25 small balls with your hands and push a whole almond into the centre of each ball. The almond should be completely covered with the fruit.

Spread out the chopped hazel nuts, almonds and pistachio nuts on a sheet of waxed paper.

Roll each ball into the nuts and cover again completely.

The fig is a popular given name to many plants and trees of the species, ficus belongs to the mulberry family. The name is generally applied to the fruit and plant of the common fig. One of the earliest fruit trees cultivated by man and most probably native to West Asia. The best figs come from Izmir in Turkey, although they do grow naturally in all countries bordering the Mediterranean.

The two main kinds of figs are either round or long. The skins can vary from dark purple or green of the fresh fruit with the inner pulp being different shades of red.

Fresh figs are the most juiciest and delicious of dessert fruits. But the bulk of the fig crops are either dried and packed in cellophane or canned and sold in supermarkets.

Date *Helawi*

Coconut *Ice Cream*

A delicious and exotic ice cream which is unbelievably simple to make.

Ingredients
150 g – 5 oz granulated sugar
300 ml – 10 fl oz water
2 x 400 ml – cans of coconut milk
300 ml – 10 fl oz double cream
2 tbsp shredded coconut

Method

Heat the sugar and water in a pan gently for ten minutes, until the sugar has dissolved. Cool completely then in a bowl, mix together with the coconut milk. Pour into a shallow container, cover and freeze for three hours. After this time ease out into a bowl and loosen with a metal spoon. Whisk with an electric mixer until smooth. In a separate bowl whisk the cream until soft peaks form, then fold gently into the mixture. Add the shredded coconut and transfer into the same container then re-freeze until completely solidified. Allow to soften for ten minutes at room temperature just before serving.

An elderly couple had become rather forgetful and had decided to take advice in order to improve their memories.

They had several meetings with a personal advisor and showed an overall improvement over the weeks. One evening as they were relaxing together the husband announced that he was going to eat ice cream and asked his wife if she'd like some too.

"Yes," she replied, "I'd like some coconut ice cream dear, but you'd better write it down, like we were told to so you won't forget."

"Oh no, there's no need, I can remember that," laughed the husband.

"But dear, I want chocolate sauce on it, so you'd better write it down so you won't forget."

"Don't worry," he replied confidently. "I can remember exactly what you want, coconut ice cream with chocolate sauce."

"But," she said, "I also want some nuts on it. PLEASE write it down or I know you'll get confused and bring me the wrong thing."

"You worry too much dear," he replied smiling. "I will get it exactly right." Saying that he disappeared in the kitchen with a smile on his face.

After almost 15 minutes he returned proudly with two plates of eggs and chips.

He handed it to her smiling but her smile froze and she looked angrily at him. "Didn't I tell you to write it down. I thought you'd get it all wrong. See how you forgot to bring the baked beans!"

Fruity *Canoes*

Very attractive and delicious fruit filled pastries. If you don't have the boat tins, you can use round patty tins instead.

Ingredients

Pastry
175 g – 6 oz plain flour
Pinch of salt
85 g – 3 oz butter
25 g – 1 oz caster sugar
1 large egg yolk
A little water

Filling
225 g – 8 oz fresh or canned fruit
(cherries, strawberries, raspberries, kiwi, mandarin oranges etc)
4 tbsp red currant jelly
1 tbsp fruit juice
150 ml – 5 fl oz double cream

Method
375°F – 190°C - Gas mark 5

Sift together the flour and the salt.

Rub in the butter until the mixture resembles fine breadcrumbs.

Add the sugar and bind everything with the water and egg yolk to form a soft dough.

Turn onto a floured surface and knead gently.

Use the pastry to line 12 boat tins, 4 x 2 inches, lightly greased.

Prick the sides and bases and bake blind for 10 minutes.

Allow to cool completely and then remove from the tins.

Arrange the fruit attractively in the cases then melt the jelly with the fruit juice over a low heat and brush over the fruit to set.

Leave until the glace has cooled and then spoon the cream into a piping back fitted with a small nozzle and decorate over the fruit.

Fruit *Delights*

This sweet is really simple to make it seems unbelievable that it is so delicious.

Ingredients

3 large apples, peeled cored and chopped
5 bananas, peeled and chopped
450 g – 1lb chopped dates
225 g – 8 oz ground nuts finely chopped
2 tsp ground cinnamon
2 tsp ground ginger
1 tbsp lemon rind
1 tbsp orange rind
3 fl oz orange juice
200 g – 7 oz powdered digestive biscuits
Desiccated coconut

Method

In a large mixing bowl combine the apples, bananas, dates, groundnuts, cinnamon, ginger and the rinds. With a fork mash everything to a paste, then add the orange juice and stir well together. Add just enough of the powdered biscuits to the mixture to make a stiff paste.

Make small balls and roll in desiccated coconut and serve.

Dried dates keep for a very long time. Those, which are pressed into blocks, are quite hard and tasteless but dates arranged in oval boxes on plastic stalks are sweeter and juicier.

This recipe includes plenty of dates- an important food for Arabic diets. Therefore the dates and nuts relationship is truly delicious in any form and compliment each other very well.

Fruit *Jelly*

Try this simple dessert and experiment with different flavours and colours of jellies. The topping can be also replaced with ice creams and thin custards. The fruit that has set within the jelly adds visual appeal.

Ingredients

115 g – 4 oz packet raspberry jelly
250 ml – 8 fl oz raspberry or cranberry juice
115 g – 4 oz fresh strawberries
115 g – 4 oz raspberries
1 large red skinned apple, cored and chopped

Method

Make the jelly according to the instructions on the packet, but add the fruit juice instead of the water. Then stir well.

Meanwhile prepare the fruit by chopping the strawberries in half and slicing the apples. When the jelly has almost set, place the fruit in a trifle dish or a fluted mould, pour the jelly over quickly. Allow to set.

When completely cold and just before serving, turn out onto a serving plate and serve with the topping of your choice or even just natural yoghurt.

Gulab *Jaman*

Gulab means rose and jaman means something like a doughnut. Feather light with the mystical flavour and scent of rose syrup. After they're fried, they are then dipped into a rose flavoured syrup and rolled in coconut.

Ingredients

3 tbsp melted ghee
2 eggs
1 large tin of condensed milk
1 tsp rose water
115 g – 4 oz semolina
3 tsp baking powder
55 g – 2 oz ground almonds
Enough self raising flour to make a soft dough
Vegetable oil for frying
Coconut for coating

Syrup

3 cups water
3 cups sugar
Pinch of ground cardammon
1 tsp rose water

Method

Whisk together the ghee, eggs and the condensed milk. Add the semolina and mix everything else together. Make a soft dough like a biscuit dough with just enough flour. Cover with a cling film and chill in the fridge for an hour or so. Meanwhile make the syrup by boiling all the ingredients together until it is of medium consistency.

Remove dough from the fridge and take small cherry sized portion.

Roll between your palms into an almost oblong shape. They will rise to almost 3 times their size so only small sizes are required. Heat the oil and fry in a medium heat, turning frequently to avoid becoming over brown.

When they are all fried, dip in the syrup and allow to soak in for a little while. Remove with a slotted spoon and roll in coconut.

Traditionally sweets would be served at the beginning of an Asian meal as a gesture of goodwill. Nowadays the custom is not prevalent and the sweet is served at the end of a meal just as a desert on a Western table.

There are quite a variety of Indian sweets available with the profuse use of crushed nuts, flours and semolina associated with a host of other exotic ingredients.

This recipe can be eaten anytime and is drier and easier to handle then its syrup laden cousin which is mostly served in restaurants.

The recipe makes a tin full, but the dough can be divided in half and frozen to be fried at a later date.

Gulab *Jaman*

Semolina *Helwa*

A quick and easy to prepare helwa.

Ingredients
115 g – 4 oz ghee
115 g – 4 oz semolina
115 g – 4 oz ground almonds
115 g – 4 oz sugar
1/2 tsp ground nutmeg
300 ml – 1/2 pt full cream milk
25 g - 1 oz raw cashew nuts, chopped

Method
Grease a large tray and set aside.

Melt the ghee in a heavy based pan over a low heat.

Add the semolina and braise slowly until golden for a few minutes, stirring continuously

Add the almonds, sugar and the nutmeg then stir again.

Add the milk and stir until the mixture thickens and comes away from the sides of the pan. Turn out the mixture onto the greased tray and spread evenly to the desired thickness. Sprinkle the cashews evenly over the top and gently press with the back of the spoon.

Allow to cool slightly and cut into squares or diamonds.

Serve when set.

Sponge *Dessert*

To this delicious iced dessert the addition of hazelnuts makes the taste supreme.

Ingredients
85 g – 3 oz shelled and chopped hazel nuts
32 sponge fingers
150 ml – 2/3 cup strong black coffee
2 tbsp milk
450 ml – 3/4 pt double cream
85 g – 3 oz sifted icing sugar
150 g – 5 oz plain chocolate &
icing sugar, cocoa to dust

Method
400°F – 200°C - Gas mark 6

Pre heat the oven then spread out the hazel nuts on a baking sheet and toast slowly in the oven for a few minutes until just golden.

Cool completely.

Line a 1.2 ltr or a 2 pint loaf tin with clear film and cut the sponge fingers to fit the base and sides.

Mix the coffee and the milk in a shallow dish and dip the sponge fingers briefly into the coffee mixture and return to the tin with the sugary side facing down.

Whip the cream with the icing sugar until it holds soft peaks.

Roughly chop 85 g - 3 oz of chocolate and fold into the cream with the hazelnuts.

Melt the remaining chocolate in a small bowl and set over a pan of simmering water. Cool then fold into the cream mixture.

Spoon into the tin. Moisten the remaining biscuits in the coffee and layer over the filling. Cover with the cling film and freeze until firm.

To serve remove from the freezer and turn out onto a serving plate 20 minutes before and dust with icing sugar and cocoa, letting some fall on the plate.

Cut into 1/2 inch slices and serve.

Honey *Sweet Bread*

A delicious sweetbread using mother natures finest ingredients.

Ingredients
1 cup honey
2 tbsp vegetable oil
1 egg
350 g – 12 oz self raising flour
1 tbsp baking powder
Pinch of salt
55 g – 2 oz chopped roasted nuts
1 cup raw wheat bran
1 cup canned pineapple juice

Method
350°F – 180°C - Gas mark 4

Pre heat a 9 x 5" loaf pan.

Blend together the honey, oil and the egg gradually and mix well at full speed for a few minutes.

Sift together the flour, baking powder and salt, then coat the nuts with one half of the flour.

Gradually fold in the other half to the egg mixture, then mix in the bran and pineapple juice.

Finally add the remaining flour and nut mixture and mix gently but well together.

Pour into a lightly greased loaf pan and bake in a pre heated oven. Allow to cool in the pan before turning out onto a cooling tray.

Serve hot or cold with honey and butter.

Honeycomb *Toffee*

This golden toffee is lighter then the ready made variety. You may substitute honey for the golden light syrup.

Ingredients
1 tsp butter
450 g – 1 lb sugar
5 fl oz water
Pinch of cream of tarter
4 fl oz golden syrup
1 tsp bicarbonate of soda
2 tbsp cold water

Method
Grease two 8 x 12" baking tins and set aside. Put the sugar, water, cream of tarter and the syrup into a heavy based pan. Cook gently over a low heat stirring occasionally with a wooden spoon. When the sugar has dissolved increase the heat to moderately high and bring the mixture to the boil. Continue boiling without stirring until the temperature reaches 310° F on a sugar thermometer, or until a small piece dropped into cold water forms a hard ball.

Remove the pan from the heat. Mix the soda with the cold water and stir it into the toffee. Continue stirring gently until the toffee has swelled up then pour into the greased tins.

Allow the toffee to cool slightly then mark into squares before it has hardened completely.

Lift out of the tin and break into squares, store in a glass jar.

Mango *Kulfi*

*A smooth delicious and refreshing kulfi.
Made with the king of fruit - the ever
popular mango.*

Ingredients
1 tbsp custard powder
3 tbsp caster sugar
3/4 pint milk
2 medium mangoes, peeled and pureed or
A can of mango pulp (15 oz)
1/4 pint of double cream, lightly whipped
Mango slices for decoration

Method

In a saucepan pour the milk then add the
custard powder and sugar. Whisk together
until no lumps remain then put to the boil
on a low heat. Continue to whisk as the
mixture warms up making sure that no
lumps are present.

Bring to the boil and let the mixture
thicken. Remove from the heat and
immediately place in a bowl of cold water,
stirring continuously.

Let the mixture cool down completely but
do not allow a skin to form. When cold,
whisk in the mango pulp or puree and the
double cream. It will look deliciously light
and airy. Pour into a suitable container
and freeze.

Remove from the freezer every 20 minutes
and whisk vigorously to prevent crystals
forming in the mixture. Repeat this
5 to 6 times.

Just before serving, allow the kulfi 10-15
minutes in the refrigerator to soften
it slightly.

Decorate with mango slices.

Marshmallow *Squares*

*Small delicious melt in the mouth confectionery.
Vegetable gelatine is available in health food
shops. Simple to make and finish by rolling in
icing sugar, toasted desiccated coconut or
coated with melted chocolate.*

Ingredients
115 g – 4 oz sifted, icing sugar
350 g – 12 oz sugar
2 tsp powdered glucose
10 fl oz water
25 g – 1 oz gelatine dissolved with 4 fl oz water
1 egg white, beaten into stiff peaks
1 tsp vanilla essence

Method

Using 25 g - 1 oz of the sifted icing sugar,
lightly dust a 20 cm - 8" square baking tin.

Put the remaining icing sugar on a large
plate and set aside.

In a large saucepan, dissolve the sugar and
glucose in the water over a low heat.

Stir constantly until the sugar has
dissolved. Then increase the heat and bring
to the boil, then allow to boil without
stirring until it has reached a temperature of
260° F on a sugar thermometer. Or until it
has reached the hard ball stage.

Remove the pan from the heat.

Put the dissolved gelatine in a large mixing
bowl, and then pour the sugar syrup over
the gelatine, stirring constantly.

Using an electric beater, beat in the egg
white and continue beating until the mixture
is stiff. Beat in the vanilla essence and spoon
the mixture into the prepared tin.

Set the tin aside to cool. When cooled
thoroughly and set, cut into 1" squares.

Lift carefully and roll into the remaining
icing sugar or toasted coconut.

Store in an airtight tin.

Mango *Kulfi*

Sugared *Diamonds*

Small sweet diamonds when you want something different with tea.

Ingredients
Dough
225 g – 8 oz plain flour
Pinch of salt
25 g – 1 oz marg
25 g – 1 oz butter
2 lightly beaten eggs
1 tbsp milk
Vegetable oil for frying

Coating
Caster sugar
Cinnamon powder
Apricot or red jam

Method
Sieve the flour and salt then rub in the margarine and butter. Add the well beaten eggs and milk and make into a soft dough.

Turn onto a lightly floured surface, and knead for about 5 minutes and mix until smooth.

Cover the dough and leave in a warm place for an hour.

Place the dough on a floured surface and roll out to a rectangle.

Fold the top third downwards and the bottom third upwards like an envelope, then give the dough a half turn.

Repeat this twice and then let the dough rest for 10 minutes.

Roll out the dough until it is a 1/4" thick, then cut into 20 diamond shapes.

Heat the oil until just hot then fry the diamonds on a moderate heat making sure they don't turn brown immediately.

Remove from the oil and drain well. Sprinkle with sugar and cinnamon powder and serve with jam whilst still warm.

Yoghurt *Cream Dessert*

A creamy cake on a crunchy biscuit base. The surprise is that it needs no baking.

Ingredients
115 g – 4 oz + 1tsp melted butter
225 g – 8 oz crushed digestive biscuits
1 tsp ground cinnamon
10 fl oz yogurt
16 fl oz double cream
1 tbsp lemon juice
55 g – 2 oz caster sugar
450 g – 1 lb finely chopped fresh apricots
1/2 oz gelatine dissolved (vegetarian gelatine is widely available)
55 g – 2 oz chocolate
55 g – 2 oz ground pistachio nuts

Method
In a medium bowl, combine the crushed biscuits, the cinnamon and 1 tsp of melted butter.

Line the base of a loose bottom round greased 9" cake tin with this mixture.

Press in firmly against the bottom of the tin.

Beat the yoghurt, half of the cream, the lemon juice and sugar with a wooden spoon.

The mixture should now be smooth and creamy.

Stir in the apricots and beat in the dissolved gelatine mixture.

Set the mixture in a fridge for 20 minutes until it is almost set.

Using a large metal spoon the mixture onto the biscuit base and place the tin in the fridge until it is totally set.

Meanwhile beat the remaining double cream until it forms stiff peaks.

Remove the cake tin and spoon the cream on the top. Swirl it with a fork to make a pattern.

Sprinkle the grated chocolate and ground pistachio over the top for decoration.

Chill and serve when required.

TIP: Gelatine can be substituted in this case with agar agar.

Nut & Pastry *Pudding*

This is a delicious and delightful pudding often made in the Middle East.

Ingredients

12 sheets filo pastry
250 ml – 9 fl oz double cream
2 tbsp rose water + 1 egg
85 g – 3 oz chopped, pistachio nuts
85 g – 3 oz chopped almonds
1 pint milk
115 g – 4 oz golden sultanas
1 tbsp cardammon powder
Single cream for serving

....

Method

375°F – 190°C - Gas mark 5

....

In a lightly buttered baking sheet, place the filo pastry and bake for about 15 minutes or until crisp.

Remove from the oven and set aside.

In a saucepan pour the milk and the cream, then heat very gently until hot but not boiling. Beat together the egg and rose water and slowly drizzle this into the pan. Continue stirring all the time until the mixture thickens.

Into a shallow baking sheet, crush some of the pastry, then layer with the nuts and sultanas. Make 2 or 3 layers like this and pour the mixture from the pan over these layers then sprinkle the cardammon powder over the top.

Bake for 20 minutes until it is a lovely golden brown.

Serve with single cream.

Filo pastry consists of a wafer like thinness and originates from the Middle East. It can be made at home but this pastry is fairly difficult and time consuming to make. It is readily available in the chilled and frozen counters of most supermarkets, continental shops and delicatessens.

Filo pastry can be used for savoury and sweet pastries, usually baked and almost identical to strudel pastry, although strudel originated in Europe.

Usually pastries require warm ingredients and light handling. But Filo pastry has to be kneaded and beaten vigorously to enable the gluten in the flour to develop strength. This is to ensure that the pastry can be stretched into a very thin resilient sheet. For the same reason strong plain flour is used as yields more gluten then normal flour. Gluten helps to produce elasticity in the dough.

The thin sheet of dough can be spread with a filling, rolled, folded or crushed.

This sweet is very common in the Middle East as well as many parts of the Mediterranean particularly Turkey.

You can of course use a combination of different nuts, which have been ground, add a variety of fillings, coconut or dried fruits.

It is simply a matter of choice and taste.

Middle Eastern *Delights*

A moist confection made with syrup, cocoa and dried fruit. Truly a taste of the East.

Ingredients
225 g – 8 oz sugar
5 fl oz water
Juice of half a lemon
115 g – 4 oz cocoa powder
175 g – 6 oz walnut finely chopped
55 g – 2 oz almonds finely chopped
55 g – 2 oz raisins
55 g – 2 oz candied peel finely chopped
55 g – 2 oz icing sugar

Method
In a large saucepan mix the sugar and water and stir over a low heat. When the sugar has dissolved completely. Increase the heat to high and boil rapidly until the temperature reaches 220° F on a sugar thermometer or until a small amount of the syrup dropped into cold water forms a ball.

Add the lemon juice, sifted cocoa powder, and all the rest of the ingredients except the icing sugar.

Stir constantly and cook the mixture on the lowest heat again and cook until it is stiff. Remove the pan from the heat and allow to cool for 5 minutes.

Meanwhile sprinkle a work surface with the icing sugar, and then scrape the mixture from the pan onto the surface.

Using your hands form into a roll about 16" long and 1.5" diameter.

Set aside to cool slightly and wrap in a greaseproof paper and chill in the fridge until firm.

Remove the roll and discard the paper, slice thinly with a sharp knife and serve.

Petit-*Fours*

What an easy way to make these petit fours. Change the coatings each time and create a different taste.

Ingredients
2 jam swiss rolls
115 g – 4 oz ground almonds
1 tsp jam
1 egg
Milk – if required
2 tbsp cocoa powder
1 tsp vanilla essence
1 tsp almond essence

Method
Crumble the swiss rolls into a large bowl. Add the almonds, cocoa powder and the two essences. Separate the egg, then add the yolk to the mixture.

Mix the ingredients well together until it is smooth and creamy. You may need the milk if it is too dry.

Roll into 20 small balls.

Whisk the egg white till frothy and dip the balls in this. Coat with any of the suggested toppings.

Drop into petit-four cases and allow to dry.

We don't really know which country the term petit four originated from. Most likely petit fours evolved over many years.

Apparently the phrase dates back to the 18th century and suggests that it was derived from the name, i.e. small ovens which were used to bake these sweet delicacies. Or maybe even the art of making them or perhaps it even meant to bake at a very low temperature.

Others suggest that the name refer to 'small bit' or even 'one bite.' No matter what the definition, each is correct to a certain point. Most probably it refers to a one or two bite morsel which is served for tea times or after a meal.

Pineapple *Ice Cream*

Take advantage of the pineapples, already picked and canned for you and make this cooling dessert.

Ingredients
4 eggs separated
55 g – 2 oz caster sugar
1/2 tsp vanilla essence
300 ml – 1/2 pt whipping cream
30 ml – 2 tbsp icing sugar
200 g – 7.5 oz pineapple chunks
85 g – 3 oz ground pistachio nuts

Method
Place the egg yolks in a bowl, then add the caster sugar and vanilla essence. Beat until very thick and pale in colour. In another bowl, whip the cream and icing sugar until they are soft peaks, and then mix in well with the egg yolk mixture.

Whisk the egg whites in a separate large bowl until they are firm and hold stiff peaks.

Then gently fold the whites into the cream mixture and blend well. Cut the pineapple into very small pieces, add the nuts and stir into the cream and mix well.

Pour the mixture into an ice cream container and freeze for a few hours until firm and set.

Take out and stir well at regular intervals.

Scoop out and serve decorated with a sprinkling of sliced toasted almonds.

The pineapple, with its magnificent crown of leaves, has always been the main rival of the mango for the title "king of fruits". It has graced the tables of the rich and famous in the West since its introduction into Europe from South America in the 17th century. The name of the fruit is derived from its superficial resemblance to the pinecone, though the two have little else in common.

The pineapple is a member of a family of tropical plants, the bromeliads, of which it is the only edible species. Today, pineapples are cultivated throughout the tropics, especially in places where the rainfall is high. The principal exporters of pineapples are Hawaii, the Ivory Coast and Dominica.

The pineapple is an unusual fruit in that it does not ripen if removed from the bush on which it grows. A day before the fruit matures sweet sap shoots from the roots into the pineapple, ripening it at once.

Only this moment is the fruit ready to be picked. It is useless to buy an unripe pineapple in the hope that it will ripen if kept in a warm place.

The best way to judge the ripeness of the fruit is to smell it. If it is ripe it should give out a sweet smell.

The outer colour gives no indication of ripeness. The crown of the leaves should be glossy, not withered or dry, and a leaf plucked from the crown should come away easily.

Pineapples are at their best during the summer months of the country in which they are grown.

Pistachio *Rolls*

Lots of exotic ingredients filled in a filo pastry. Your guests will reach for them again and again.

Ingredients

200 g – 7 oz ground pistachio nuts
55 g – 2 oz ground almonds
55 g – 2 oz caster sugar
1 tbsp rose water
1/2 tsp ground cinammon
12 sheets filo pastry
115 g – 4 oz melted butter
Icing sugar for dusting

Method

325 °F – 160 °C - Gas mark 3

Make the filling by mixing together the ground nuts, sugar, cinnamon and rose water.

Cut each sheet of filo pastry into four rectangles, taking care to cover the others with a damp cloth.

Brush the rectangles with a little melted butter and place a teaspoon of filling in the centre. Fold in the sides and roll up sealing the edge well.

Follow the same method until all the rolls are ready.

Place all the rolls on a buttered baking sheet and bake in a pre heated oven for about 30 minutes or until lightly golden.

Remove carefully and cool on a cooling tray finally dusting with icing sugar.

Quick *Dessert*

Delightfully simple to make and in minutes. My eldest son Rizwaan enjoys making and serving this divine dessert.

Ingredients

6 bananas (or any other soft fruit) peeled and sliced
115 g – 4 oz strawberries, hulled and halved
16 fl oz double cream
175 g – 6 oz sugar
4 tbsp water
2 tbsp rose water

Method

Arrange the fruit in a medium sized glass dish.

Spread the cream over the fruit and level the surface.

Cover and chill the dish in the fridge for 30 minutes.

In a heavy saucepan, dissolve the water and sugar over a low heat stirring constantly.

Increase the heat to medium high and bring the syrup to the boil.

Boil for 10 minutes without stirring or until it is golden in colour.

Add the rose water and remove the pan from the heat and immerse the base in a large bowl of cold water for 10 seconds.

Pour this syrup over the cream slowly.

Serve immediately or return to the fridge until it is required.

Pistachio *Kulfi*

A simple recipe for the ever popular kulfi, otherwise known as Indian ice cream.

Ingredients

5 fl oz fresh milk
2 tbsp ground rice
1 tbsp ground almonds
14.5 oz tin evaporated milk
1 level tsp ground cardammon
55 g – 2 oz sugar
15 fl oz double cream
1 tbsp rosewater or 6 drops of any other flavour such as vanilla, almond, etc.
25 g – 1 oz unsalted pistachio nuts, shelled and lightly crushed

Method

Heat the milk until it is just warm. Mix the ground rice and almonds into a bowl. Gradually add the warmed milk a little at a time, making a thin paste of pouring consistency. Make sure that there are no lumps.

Heat the evaporated milk to boiling point and add the ground cardamom. Take the pan off the heat and gradually add the almond and rice mixture, stirring continuously.

Add the sugar and cream. Place the pan over medium heat. Let the mixture simmer for about 15 minutes, stirring all the time. Remove the pan from the heat and allow to cool slightly. Add the flavouring and half of the pistachio nuts. Mix well.

Allow the mixture to cool completely, stirring frequently to prevent froth forming.

Pack into ice cream tubs or individual moulds. Top with the remaining pistachio nuts and freeze. Allow to defrost slightly in the refrigerator before serving.

Ice cream - a Chinese invention - was introduced by Arabs and Persians to the Middle East. But it was Marco Polo who brought the dessert to Italy in the 13th century.

Hand cranked churning pails were used to make the sweet at home with a frozen mixture of ice and salt. This increased in popularity after the turn of the century in Europe and the Commonwealth.

However, long before all this happened, a frozen dessert was developed in Delhi, either brought to the country by the Moguls from Kabul or originated by them in India. This was kulfi, which derived its name from the conical metal device in which it was made. Manuscripts of the sixteenth century describe the preparation of kulfi in Emperor Akbar's royal kitchen as freezing a mixture of milk solids, pistachio nuts and saffron essence in conical metal receptacles and sealing the contents. Kulfi has been made and sold on the streets of every major city in India for centuries. It is firmer than conventional ice cream and is usually set in small aluminium cone-shaped moulds. However, today, plastic ice cream tubs can be used instead. Try this recipe but be adventurous by substituting one fruit for another, creating your own formulas and flavours.

An abundance of fruit is available to give a wide range of tastes.

The fruit should always be pulverised but a little should be saved for decoration.

A selection *of Kulfi's*

Tapioca *Pudding*

A nourishing and attractive dessert with the addition of apples. Delicious served hot or cold.

Ingredients

16 fl oz milk
55 g – 2 oz tapioca
1 tbsp butter
55 g – 2 oz sugar
Pinch of allspice
1 tsp grated lemon rind
2 egg yolks
2 egg whites, stiffly beaten
450 g – 1 lb roughly chopped cooking apples
Pinch of nutmeg
55 g – 2 oz raisins
2 tbsp soft brown sugar

Method

350°F – 180°C - Gas mark 4

Warm the milk in a heavy based pan. When it has almost reached boiling point, sprinkle in the tapioca and boil for about 10 minutes. Stir frequently until the mixture thickens. Grease a 3 pt oven proof dish with a little butter and pre heat the oven.

When the milk mixture has thickened add the butter, allspice, sugar, and lemon rind and cook for a few minutes more until the sugar has dissolved. Remove the pan from the heat and stir in the egg yolks, then carefully with a metal spoon stir in the stiff egg whites. Spread the apples in the dish and then sprinkle the raisins, brown sugar and nutmeg over the apples. Spoon the tapioca mixture over the apples carefully covering all the apples. Bake for about half an hour in the oven or until the top is firm and golden brown.

Remove from the oven and serve hot with additional single cream if desired.

Tapioca is a form of starch which is extracted from the roots of the cassava plant. This is a small shrub of which there are some 2000 varieties. Cassava grows in tropical regions but is a native of Asia and South America. During the 1800's Spanish explorers took it to the East Indies and then from there it spread quickly to Africa and other regions. The tapioca is drawn from the root of the plant, which becomes stringy when mixed with water. The sap is extracted and dropped into hot plates where it gelatinises into the characteristic white balls of starch. Tapioca is used as a thickener in puddings and swells and becomes very clear when boiled in a liquid, making it perfect to use in milk and milk based puddings or thickened desserts. It is most commonly sold in the pearl form.

Banana *Pudding*

A simply irresistible and very quick pudding, using any flavoured cake. Here it's teamed up with ginger cake to draw out some mystical hidden flavours.

Ingredients

4 thick slices of ginger cake
6 sliced bananas
2 tbsp lemon juice
300 ml – 1/2 pt whipping cream
4 tbsp fruit juice
3 tbsp soft brown sugar

Method

Break up the cake into chunks and arrange in an oven proof pudding dish.
Slice the bananas and sprinkle the lemon juice over them. Whip the cream and when firm gently whip in the fruit juice. Fold in the bananas and pour this mixture over the cake then top with the sugar.

Place under a hot grill for a few minutes to caramelise.

Chill to set and serve hot as required.

Lime *Dessert*

This dessert is a speciality, which will be sure to delight with its tangy flavour.

Ingredients
115 g – 4 oz + 1 tsp unsalted, melted butter
225 g – 8 oz crushed digestive biscuits
85 g – 3 oz caster sugar
4 egg yolks
15 fl oz sweetened condensed milk
5 fl oz fresh lime juice
10 fl oz double cream
Ground nuts for decoration

Method

Lightly grease a loose bottom round 23 cm - 9" tin with the teaspoon of melted butter.

Combine the biscuits, sugar and butter in a bowl.

Lightly press this mixture into the prepared cake tin.

Cover with aluminium foil and chill in the fridge for an hour.

Meanwhile make the filling in a large mixing bowl, by beating the egg yolks until they are thick and creamy.

Add the condensed milk and lime juice and beat until the mixture is frothy.

Put this into the tin and place again in the fridge to set for a few hours.

In a smaller bowl whip the double cream and remove the pin carefully from the cake tin and slide onto a serving plate.

Spread the cream thickly over the top.

Decorate as you like and serve immediately.

It's not surprising that so much honour has been given to citrus fruits.

The mere mention sends the palette in search of this sparkling juice and its sweet aftermath. But the pleasures are not in the taste alone, it's also in the fragrance.

The aroma comes from oils present in the rind.

Hasn't nature been generous in lavishing us with these lemon yellows, orange tones and lime greens? Citrus fruits belong to the family of Rutacea.

They contain an abundance of Vitamin C.

Vitamin C is the vitamin that keeps you upright despite the ever - revolving germs, pollution and infections circulating in today's world.

A glass of freshly squeezed orange juice for breakfast does wonders for you. Sweet lime has practically no acidic content and in Northern India is widely used as a remedy for fever connected to malaria because its juices contain therapeutic properties.

Among other uses of these fruits is the rind. Abundantly used for baking purposes adding flavour to your cakes, biscuits and desserts.

Triple *Delight*

The dough for these attractive and colourful biscuits can be stored in the fridge and baked freshly as and when required. Serve them after dinner with cappuccino or coffee to replace the dessert.

Ingredients
115 g – 4 oz butter
115 g – 4 oz sugar
1 egg
225 g – 8 oz plain flour
2 tsp baking powder
Pinch of salt
1 tbsp instant coffee powder-dissolved in
3 tsp hot water
1/2 tsp vanilla essence
1 tbsp grated orange rind
1 tsp green food colouring
1 tbsp chopped angelica

Method
400 °F – 200 °C - Gas mark 6

Beat the butter with a wooden spoon until it is light and fluffy then add the sugar and beat the mixture until it's creamy. Carry on beating and add the egg to this mixture.

Add the sifted flour and salt then with a large metal spoon fold in all together.

With your hands lightly knead the dough into three equal pieces.

Place each piece in small mixing bowls.

With a metal spoon stir the coffee mixture into 1/3 of the dough.

In the second dough add the vanilla essence and the orange rind.

Stir the green colouring and candied angelica into the third piece of dough.

Knead each dough until smooth.

Wrap in greaseproof paper and chill for an hour in the fridge.

Remove and roll out each piece into oblong shapes. Place each dough on top of the other and roll tightly like a swiss roll.

Slice in 1/4" thickness, arrange on a greased baking tray. Bake in a pre-heated oven for 10 minutes.

Cool on a wire tray.

Creamy *Fruit Dessert*

Such a light, creamy and delicious dessert that can be made minutes before serving.

Ingredients
4 ripe bananas
4 passion fruit
5 fl oz cream

Method
Mash the bananas until it becomes a thick puree.

Cut two of the passion fruit in half and scoop out the pulp.

Mix with the bananas and cream.

Transfer into tall serving dishes and decorate with the pulp from the remaining passion fruit.

Chill for 30 minutes before serving.

Little *Rolls*

Sweet little filled rolls and very attractive too with the cherries.

Ingredients
125 g – 5 oz butter
300 g – 10 oz self raising flour
Pinch of salt
Few drops of vanilla essence
6 tbsp caster sugar
1 tsp baking powder
2 eggs
Coconut

Filling
85 g – 3 oz butter
1 tsp vanilla essence
175 g – 6 oz coconut
55 g – 2 oz icing sugar
55 g – 2 oz coloured cherries

Method
350°F – 180°C - Gas mark 4

Rub the butter into the flour, baking powder and salt.

Add the sugar and the vanilla. Beat together the eggs and take 2/3rds and use this to make a soft biscuit dough.

Roll out to 5 mm thick then cut into small rectangles.

Spoon the filling into the triangle and roll up sealing the edges well. Dip into the beaten egg and roll in coconut. Decorate with the small pieces of cherries.

Place on a lightly greased baking sheet and bake for 15 minutes.

Leave for a few minutes on the sheet before transferring and cooling on a wire tray.

Make the filling by blending together the butter and the icing sugar. Then add the rest of the ingredients. Leave the cherries for decorating.

Carrot *Helwa*

Delicious and naturally colourful Helwa made with the simplest method using basic everyday ingredients.

Ingredients
400 g – 14 oz sugar
3 tbsp water
450 g – 1 lb grated carrots
Few strands of saffron
1/2 tsp chopped, fresh root ginger
85 g – 3 oz finely chopped almonds
25 g – 1 oz ground pistachio
Pinch of cardammon powder
2 tbsp lemon juice

Method
In a medium heavy based pan, dissolve the sugar in the water stirring constantly on a low heat.

Stir in the carrots and saffron, when the sugar has dissolved completely increase the heat and boil rapidly for around 30 minutes until the mixture has thickened.

Remove the pan from the heat and add the almonds, ginger and lemon juice.

Stir the mixture well and pour into a lightly greased baking sheet and sprinkle the cardammon powder and pistachio powder over then allow to cool.

Cut into squares and leave to set.

Walnut *Rolls*

These rolls have a wonderful flaky texture filled with a rich walnut mixture. A delicious treat at any time.

Ingredients
300 g – 10 oz strong, plain flour
7 g – 1/4 oz plain dry yeast
3 tbsp caster sugar
Grated rind of one lemon
1 small well beaten egg
40 g – 1.5 oz unsalted melted butter
120 ml – 4 fl oz warm milk
2 small egg yolks and granulated sugar for sprinkling

Filling
115 g – 4 oz walnuts finely grounded
1 tsp cinnamon powder
55 g – 2 oz caster sugar
2 small egg whites

Method
325°F – 170°C - Gas mark 3

Warm the mixing bowl before sifting in the flour and then stir in the dry yeast.

Make a well in the centre and stir in the sugar, lemon rind, egg, melted butter and the milk. Knead well, adding a little extra liquid or flour as required to make a smooth but not sticky dough. On a lightly floured surface, knead this dough and roll out thinly into a rectangle approx. 18 x 12 inches. Cut into six squares.

Mix the walnuts, cinnamon and sugar with the egg whites and divide equally among the squares. Take care to leave the edges clean and then carefully roll up each square diagonally from one corner to another to form a long roll. Curl these rolls into a crescent shape and place on a greased baking sheet. Cover with a cling film and leave in a warm place to rise. It will take almost 2 hours before the rolls have risen.

Brush with the whisked egg yolks and sprinkle with sesame seeds, or pine nuts.

Place in a pre heated oven, bake until lightly golden then just before serving sprinkle with some icing sugar.

Cherry *Candies*

Very attractive sweets which are ideal for children's parties. Try looking at health stores for the coloured cherries to give a jewelled effect.

Ingredients
55 g – 2 oz butter
115 g – 4 oz sifted icing sugar
1-2 tsp hot water
Few drops of vanilla essence
Few drops of rose pink colouring
A little icing sugar for rolling
Glace cherries for decoration

Method
Melt the butter in a large pan over a low heat. When melted remove from the heat and pour in the icing sugar with 1 tsp of hot water. Add the essence and food colouring and beat well. If the mixture is too sweet then add the other 1 tsp of hot water. Leave to cool.

Sprinkle a little icing sugar onto a clean board and tip the mixture out onto it.

Divide into two and make two rolls about an inch in diameter.

Wrap in cling film and chill till firm.

Remove from the fridge and slice each of the two rolls into thin slices (about 12 slices each) and decorate with chopped pieces of cherries.

Yeast *Doughnuts*

These doughnuts are delicious with home made jam such as plum or strawberry. Best eaten whilst still fresh and warm.

Ingredients
225 g – 8 oz strong white flour
1/2 tsp salt
7 g – 1/4 oz sachet dried yeast
1 well beaten egg
4 – 6 tbsp milk
1 tbsp granulated sugar
4 tbsp jam
Oil for deep frying
55 g – 2 oz caster sugar
1/2 tsp cinnamon powder

Method
Sift the flour into a bowl which has been warmed.

Stir in the yeast and make a well. Add the egg, warmed milk and sugar.

Mix together well to form a soft dough adding a little more milk if necessary to make a smooth dough. Beat well and cover with a cling film. Leave for almost two hours in a warm place. By then it should have risen well to almost double it's size.

Knead the dough on a lightly floured surface and divide into ten.

Shape each into a round ball and make a hole where you put a tsp of jam in the centre. Dampen the edges of the dough with water and then form a ball, press firmly to ensure the edges won't open up during frying.

Place on a lightly greased baking sheet and leave to rise for 15 minutes.

Heat the oil in a large wok or pan and when just hot turn onto a medium heat and fry the doughnuts gently for 5-8 minutes until golden brown.

Drain on a kitchen towel.

Mix the caster sugar and cinnamon on a plate and roll the doughnuts into this whilst still warm.

A policeman pulls a hockey player over for speeding and asks him to get out of the car. After eyeing the man carefully he asks, "Sir, I couldn't help but notice that your eyes are bloodshot. Have you been drinking?"

The famous hockey player was really upset at this question and immediately replies, "Officer, I couldn't help but notice that your eyes are glazed. Have you been eating doughnuts?"

Children's *Pudding*

This pudding is a favourite with children. The delicious chocolate sauce will collect at the bottom of the dish as the sponge cake is baking.

Ingredients
55 g – 2 oz butter
85 g – 3 oz caster sugar
2 eggs, separated
350 ml – 12 fl oz milk
40 g – 1.5 oz self raising flour
5 tsp cocoa powder

Method
350°F – 180°C - Gas Mark 4

Cream the butter and sugar together in a bowl until it is light and fluffy.

Beat in the egg yolks and stir in the milk. Sift together the flour and cocoa powder over the creamed mixture then beat well together.

Whisk the egg whites until very stiff then fold into the mixture. Pour into a one litre oven proof dish. Bake in a pre heated oven for 40 minutes.

The top of the pudding must have set and will spring back when touched lightly.

Best eaten hot with the separated sauce spooned over the top.

Vermicelli *Helwa*

Similar to those of the Arab and Lebanese sweets and very simple to make. All it needs are a few ingredients and about 20 minutes of your time.

Ingredients
200 g – 7 oz roasted vermicelli strands
1 x 405 g tin of condensed milk
115 g – 4 oz desiccated coconut
115 g – 4 oz almonds and pistachio nuts
250 g – 8 oz butter

Method
Crush the vermicelli into a bowl.

In a heavy based pan melt the butter throwing in the vermicelli at the same time.

Stir continuously on a low heat until all the butter has melted and taking care not to burn the vermicelli.

To this add the nuts and desiccated coconut and stir again until well mixed.

Finally add the condensed milk and almost immediately turn the cooker off.

You must be careful not to burn the milk and keep stirring away from the heat.

Pour out into a greased thali or tray and sprinkle with a little desiccated coconut almonds and pistachio nuts.

Cut into diamond shapes whilst still warm and serve when cold and firm.

The ingredients of sweets and helwa include a rich concoction ranging from ghee, almonds, pistachio, saffron and even semolina and crushed vermicelli.

Whilst almonds and pistachios play an important role in the main body of the sweets as well as for decoration, the rose water and saffron contribute toward the fragrance. Most sweets are milk based and the inclusion of condensed milk, sugar is omitted.

Vermicelli is a variety of Italian pasta, which is extruded through very small holes and then dried. In appearance it is like strands, very fine ones and brown in colour.

I really don't want to put you off, but it is always interesting to know where the words are derived from, and I am sorry to say that the literal translation of vermicelli is "little worms!"

Mango *Dessert*

This delightful dessert is simple to make and very delicious.

Ingredients
1 ripe mango
1 tbsp lemon juice
225 g – 8 oz raspberries
Caster sugar, just enough to taste
2 egg whites
150 ml – 5 fl oz whipping cream

Method
Peel the mango and cut away the flesh from the centre stone and place in a bowl.

Sprinkle over the lemon juice. Set aside a few raspberries for decoration and add the remainder to the mango and puree together in a processor.

Continue until smooth and press through a sieve into a large bowl and sweeten to taste. Whisk the egg whites stiffly and then whip the cream into soft peaks, fold them both gently into the fruit puree.

When well blended spoon into tall glasses, cover with cling film and chill.

Serve decorated with the reserved raspberries.

**Tip: If fresh mangoes are not available, use the tinned variety or two large fresh peaches.

Vermicelli *Helwa*

Sweets & Desserts

Hazelnut *Toffee*

Quick, easy and fun to make. The hazelnuts can be replaced by peanuts for a change.

Ingredients
115 g – 4 oz butter
115 g – 4 oz hazel nuts
115 g – 4 oz soft brown sugar
4 fl oz golden syrup
1/2 cup light corn syrup
1 tsp vanilla essence

Method
350°F – 180°C - Gas mark 4

In a heavy pan melt the butter, and add the hazelnuts, sugar, syrup and vanilla over a moderate heat.

Stir until the sugar has dissolved.

Bring the mixture to the boil and continue stirring frequently until it reaches 275° F on a sugar thermometer.

Be careful not to let the mixture brown.

Remove the pan from the heat and pour the toffee into a greased tray.

Wait until slightly cooked and almost, but not set completely.

Mark with a sharp knife and into required sizes. When completely set, lift out and snap into slices and store in an airtight tin or bottle.

The Hazel is a small brown nut with a hard brown shell.

It's partly covered with a lobed husk and grows in clusters on a tree.

Rich in oil and with a distinctive taste. Widely used for the inclusion in baking as well as chocolates. Hazelnuts grow in many parts of Britain, although Kent is well recognised for growing the nut for commercial purposes.

Other countries where they are imported from are the United States, France, Italy, Spain and Turkey.

Hazelnut *Whirls*

These biscuits make a delicious treat with hot tea or coffee. The method is different from other biscuits.

Ingredients
55 g – 2 oz unsalted butter
115 g – 4 oz self raising flour
1 egg
1/2 tsp vanilla essence
175 g – 6 oz ground hazelnuts
85 g – 3 oz caster sugar
55 g – 2 oz ground pistachio nuts.

Method
300°F – 150°C - Gas mark 2

Beat together the butter and flour until light and creamy.

Using a metal spoon fold in the lightly beaten egg, nuts, sugar and vanilla essence.

On a lightly floured surface, roll into 1/8" thick

Using a pastry cutter, cut in 40 circles.

Place in a lightly greased baking sheet and press a few ground pistachio nuts for decoration. Cook for about 25 minutes until light golden.

Remove from the oven and allow the biscuits to cool.

No Bake *Squares*

A Middle Eastern favourite made with an unusual combination of nuts, raisins and apples. Easy enough for the kids to handle and delicious for all to appreciate.

Ingredients

55 g – 2 oz pine nuts
1 apple peeled and grated
115 g – 4 oz ground almonds
115 g – 4 oz brown sugar
1 tbsp grated lemon rind
1 tsp ground cinnamon
1 tsp ground all spice
3 tbsp lemon juice
115 g – 4 oz seedless raisins
55 g – 2 oz powdered biscuits

Method

In a large mixing bowl, combine all the ingredients together.

Mash together with a fork and then press the mixture into a shallow baking tin.

Using a knife, slice into squares. Cover with cling film and cool in the fridge for an hour. Serve when thoroughly chilled.

The idea of working with the children in the kitchen might sound quite alarming but you can make it enjoyable.

The conversations that take place as they are busy in preparing the food are rather comical. You can't help but smile and wonder where children get their ideas from!

Baking and cooking are enjoyable and relaxing pastimes. Pass on these skills to your children, think of it as a valuable inheritance. In turn, they will appreciate even more the time and the effort, that you put into the preparation of all those wonderful foods you present to them, day after day. Always with a great deal of pleasure!

There are many simple yet delicious recipes, in this book which children can try and believe me, they are very proud of their hard labour. However, it is important to supervise children at all times. Cooking on the stove should be taken over by an adult without making it too obvious. Keep the conversation flowing so they don't realise your intervention. Involve and encourage the children to read the recipe on their own and follow the simple instructions. There are so many skills that can be learnt by cooking a simple recipe. Reading, measuring, and research when you pretend not to know what the ingredient is so that they can look it up.

What would be a pleasant surprise is when you are presented these simple fruits of their labour on Mother's or Father's day.

I couldn't help but smile when Junaid, my youngest son offered me a slice on Mother's day asking innocently, "mum, when's kids day?" I thought kids day was every day!

One *for the kids!*

Index

Index

The *Author*

Hajra Makda demonstrates and teaches the art of baking and cooking at various National and International venues.

She works closely with various food companies as a freelance consultant advising on recipe development and packaging design.

She contributes and submits regular articles to various publications at home and abroad and has made several television appearances.

Spice*'n'Easy*

This beautifully produced book contains a mix of 130 recipes, full colour photography and illustrations all within an intricate border.

Hajra shares a delicious and tantalising selection of traditional, cultural, classic recipes. The recipes are devised to tempt the taste buds across generations and cultures.

Discover a whole new attitude to cooking and eating as you create entire meals or sample delicious savouries and sweets.

For the more adventurous there's a chapter on International cuisine offering a sampling of food from Africa, the Middle East and the Mediterranean amongst others.

The book contains over 130 delicious to eat, enticing and aromatic recipes cooked in the shortest time possible. All with maximum flavour and visual appeal.

ISBN 0 9535617 0 4   *Price £6.99*   **www.sweetnspicy.com**

ZUMO ZEST & JUICES *are pure products made from the highest quality lemons, limes and oranges.*

Frozen quickly to preserve their natural quality and thoroughly recommended to enhance the flavour in baking and culinary uses. Perfect for cakes, biscuits, desserts and even meat and fish dishes.

Individual or larger quantities available directly only from

F A Young Farm Produce - Tel: 01761 470523